CHINESE-AMERICANS VIEW THEIR MENTAL HEALTH

PETER W. CHEN

San Francisco, California
1977

Published By

R & E RESEARCH ASSOCIATES, INC.
4843 Mission Street, San Francisco 94112

Publishers

Robert D. Reed and Adam S. Eterovich

Library of Congress Card Catalog Number
77-081019

I.S.B.N.

0-88247-476-6

TABLE OF CONTENTS

Chapter

> Introduction
> An Historical Preface
> Chinese-Americans Today
> Statement of the Problem
> Survey of the Literature

> Purpose of the Study
> Research Questions
> Assumptions
> Definitions of Major Terms
> The Research Design
> Selection of the Sample
> Source of Data
> Research Instrument
> Pretest
> Data Analysis

> Personal Characteristics
> Occupational Situations
> Educational History
> Financial and Housing Conditions

Chapter

LIST OF TABLES

LIST OF FIGURES

ACKNOWLEDGMENTS

I would like to express my deep appreciation to Dr. Robert W. Roberts, Committee Chairman, for his genuine interest, support, and guidance of this study. Professor Roberts lived through every phase of the process with me and also gave me valuable suggestions and immense assistance in all dimensions of my dissertation. Thus, he deserves much of the credit for this study. Special appreciation is also extended to Drs. Carl M. Shafer and Samuel H. Taylor, Committee members, for their invaluable help throughout the formulation and completion of this research.

Special thanks are due to Drs. Sharon Moriwaki, Marvin Karno, and Helen Northen, and my classmate, Lawrence Koseki who helped me greatly in the conceptualization and organization of this study. I am especially grateful to Bong-ho Mok, Margaret Leong, John Moy, Sylma Mui, and my wife, Lai-wah, who willingly served as interviewers in this field survey. The one hundred participants of this study deserve special acknowledgment, because without their cooperation this research would not have been possible.

I am indebted to Jon Wong, M.D., for his detailed reading and important editorial comments of the manuscript in its semifinal form. Appreciation for spontaneous assistance is also due to many of my colleagues at the South Central Mental Health Regional Services of the County of Los Angeles. Gratitude is specially attributed to the Regional Chief, Harold R. Schuman, MD., for his continuous administrative support which helped to speed up the completion of my study.

A special note of thanks goes to my parents, General and Mrs. Mao-chuan Chen, for their encouragement and interest in my doctoral study.

Finally, I wish to express my deep gratitude to my wife and children, Mei-chuang and Mei-hui, who have tolerated the ordeal of doctoral study without complaint and without their understanding and support my achievement would not have been possible.

CHAPTER I

CHINESE-AMERICANS AND MENTAL HEALTH

Introduction

This study was generated by a concern with the low utilization rate of community mental health services among Chinese-Americans in Los Angeles County. Given the paucity of knowledge about the relationship between Chinese-Americans and the mental health service system and the probable underutilization of current community mental health services by this ethnic group, this study had two major objectives: the first objective was to gain a familiarity with and an understanding of Chinese-Americans' views of mental health--including their definition of mental illness, the methods they use or prescribe for coping with mental illness, their attitudes toward and knowledge about existing mental health services, and their perceptions of barriers to receiving community mental health services. The second objective was to look for relationships between the cultural orientations of Chinese-Americans and the above-mentioned variables.

It was expected that this investigation would provide some empirical baseline data and initial insights into the perceived needs, attitudes, and knowledge among a specific Asian group that has exhibited a conspicuously low rate of utilizing community mental health services. Furthermore, it was hoped that the data gathered from this field survey would (1) lead to the formulation of hypotheses for future studies; (2) provide a theoretical framework to explore the relationships between mental health perceptions, attitudes, knowledge, and underutilization; and (3) suggest changes in mental health practice with Chinese-Americans or other related ethnic groups.

An Historical Preface

The exact date of the arrival of the first Chinese immigrant to the United States is uncertain. Bancroft, the

1

American historian, maintained that the Chinese were ship-builders in lower California from 1571 to 1748.[1] Another historian, Meany, stated that the Chinese laborers were employed in the Far West in 1788[2] Other records indicate that a group of Chinese took part in the memorial service for President Zachary Taylor as well as in the celebration of California joining the Union as a free state in 1850.[3]

Large scale immigration, however, did not begin until the California gold rush and the construction of the Central Pacific Railroad in the 1850s. These events provided the incentive for the Chinese to seek employment in this country. Since cheap white labor was extremely scarce, the Chinese became the primary labor resource for a wide variety of jobs. The Chinese were seen as industrious, thrifty, decent, and adaptable to various kinds of employment--ready and willing to perform as hard laborers for their employers. They were satisfied with low wages and were cooperative with their employers.

The Chinese were not a migrating people, particularly to foreign lands. It was considered an act of unfilial piety for a son to travel far away when his parents were still alive. However, after the Opium War had ended (1839-1840), there was the outbreak of the Taiping Rebellion (1850-1854). Both Wars badly damaged the southern provinces, especially Canton. The horrors of war, together with the population pressures, plundering, famine, caused many Chinese to seek refuge in foreign lands. Since Canton was the first Chinese port opened for foreign trade, the Cantonese were exposed to Western influences and became the first emigrants to America.[4]

The contract coolie trade started in the late 1850s. China was seen as having an inexhaustible supply of inexpensive manpower and thousands of Chinese were shipped off to Peru, Cuba, the United States, and other countries. Poor and unskilled Chinese did not understand much about the working conditions in the United States and had been induced to migrate as part of the coolie trade.

---

[1] H. H. Bancroft, History of California, 1860-1890 (San Francisco: Bancroft and Co., 1895), p. 335.

[2] E. S. Meany, History of the State of Washington (New York: The Macmillan Co., 1909), p. 26.

[3] Theodore H. Hitell, History of California (San Francisco: N. J. Stone and Co., 1897), p. 99.

[4] S. W. Kung, Chinese in American Life (Seattle: University of Washington Press, 1962), pp. 5-7.

When the Chinese arrived in this country, they started to work under "coolie contracts" for long terms of service in mining camps, on farms, and on the railroads. Their living and working conditions were no less fearful and horrible than those of the slaves from Africa. They were usually bound for seven or eight years at a salary of eighteen to twenty dollars a year. At the end of their contracts, they were freed. But by the time they had gained their freedom, many of them were either old, or physically or emotionally disabled. Some of them died of diseases brought about by the kind of work they did and suicides were not uncommon among them.[5]

It was also the time of industrialization and intensive urbanization in this country and the demand for docile and industrious laborers to work in farming, manufacturing, and industries was great. Chinese labor plotted and planted the vast fruit regions of the Sacramento Valley, the San Joaquin Valley, and much of the rest of California's agricultural domain. The Chinese also introduced into California the planting of rice, tea, and sugar cane. They were also hired as vegetable gardeners.[6]

In addition to agriculture, the Chinese worked in the manufacture of boots, brooms, matches, cigars, sugar, and other necessities. Chinese fishermen were the forerunners of the large California fishing industry. Many Chinese were employed in service occupations, working as cooks, laundrymen, and so forth.

After the construction of the railroads and the exhaustion of mines, there was a surplus of labor in this country. Increased economic competition led to anti-Chinese sentiments. Cruel persecution, antagonistic political platforms, and discriminatory legislation were adopted against the Chinese.[7] However, they were not driven out of the country. Through perserverance and difficult struggles, they began to form their own organizations and communities, known as the family associations and Chinatowns, to meet their survival needs. It was under these conditions that the early Chinese immigrants gradually settled in this country.

The Chinese population increased very rapidly in the United States. According to official sources, there were only

_____

[5]Alexander McLeod, Pigtails and Gold Dust (Caldwell, Idaho: The Caxton Printers, Ltd., 1947), pp. 70-76.

[6]H. H. Bancroft, Bancroft's Works, Vol. 38 (San Francisco: The History Co., 1890), p. 345.

[7]Bok-Lim C. Kim, "Asian-Americans: No Model Minority," Social Work 18 (May 1973): 46-47.

three Chinese in the United States in 1830; this increased to eight in 1840, 758 in 1850, 34,933 in 1860, and 105,465 in 1880.[8] The 1890 Census indicated that the total number of Chinese-Americans was 107,488.[9] The slow increase between 1880 and 1890 (2,023) is explained by the Chinese Exclusion Act of 1882. From 1890 to 1920 the Chinese population sharply decreased to 61,639.[10] Without much doubt, the decrease can be traced directly or indirectly to the anti-Chinese movement.

Later, however, the Chinese population began to increase again and rose to 74,954 in 1930.[11] The major reason for this growth was the increase of American-born Chinese. This second group of Chinese, who were raised in the United States, differ in many ways from their immigrant parents. In general, they have had greater educational and career opportunities. They also have become socially aware of the many contradictions in this country and some have sought redress of their grievances in a militant fashion.

The third group of Chinese are those who came to the United States after World War II. They were refugees, students, relatives of American citizens, and professional people. They emigrated from various areas of Asia with Chinese origins, including mainland China, Taiwan, Hong Kong, Thailand, etc. According to the U.S. Census the Chinese population had increased from 237,292 in 1960 to 435,000 in 1970.[12] A part of this growth is simply a reflection of the general population increase, but at least two-thirds of the increase can be attributed to new immigrants. The rapid increase of these people has produced a further change in the population composition as well as the social structure of the Chinese in this country.

Chinese-Americans Today

The following section reports major social indicators on Chinese-Americans from national census data. The purpose is

---

[8] U.S. Department of Commerce, Bureau of the Census, Census of the United States: 1830-1880, Population.

[9] Ibid., 1890, Population.

[10] Ibid., 1920, Population.

[11] Ibid., 1930, Population.

[12] Ibid., 1970, Population.

to document the large social needs of this ethnic population, thus supporting the assumption that Chinese-Americans underutilize community mental health and other social services.

According to the 1970 Census, 57 percent of Chinese-Americans are males and 47 percent are females. The Chinese have a very high proportion of husband and wife families-- 89 percent. Eighteen percent of all Chinese families are extended families; this is one and a half times more extended families than is found among the general population. Eleven percent of the Chinese families contain three or more generations; this is contrasted with 7 percent for the total U.S. population. While a quarter of all families in the United States consist of five or more members, 35 percent of Chinese families have so many members. The average Chinese family contains 4.0 persons compared to 3.5 persons among the white families.[13]

Of all Chinese men, 41 percent earn an annual income of less than $4,000 (31 percent for all males in the country). This is a serious problem and consequently almost half (48 percent) of Chinese wives are employed as compared to 39 percent of women in the total population. Of the Chinese families, 60 percent have more than one wage earner, while in the total population, it is only 51 percent. As a result, although individual incomes of the Chinese are below the U.S. average, the median Chinese family income in 1970 was $1,000 higher than the U.S. average.[14]

In comparison to the rest of the population, fewer Chinese families receive social security benefits (14 percent to 20 percent). Moreover, the average amount of Social Security income that Chinese families receive is lower than that of families in the total population.[15]

The national rate of poverty among the Chinese families is about 10 percent, which is close to the rate of 11 percent for the entire United States. However, only one out of 2.8 Chinese families in poverty receives public welfare. The rate for the total population is one to every 2.1. Furthermore, the proportion of Chinese families in poverty who receive public

---

[13] U.S. Department of Health, Education, and Welfare, A Study of Selected Socio-Economic Characteristic of Ethnic Minorities Based on the 1970 Census, vol. 2, Asian-Americans (Arlington, Va.: Urban Associates, Inc., July 1974), pp. vii-viii.

[14] Ibid., p. 112.

[15] Ibid., p. xi.

welfare is even lower in urban areas, particularly in New York, where only one out of four such families receive welfare assistance.[16]

Nationally, about 28 percent of all the Chinese elderly are poor. In San Francisco, it is 31 percent. The proportion is even higher in New York, where the elderly poor reach 40 percent. Most of these are males who were early immigrants and remained unmarried and childless.[17]

The housing conditions of the Chinese in the United States are poor and overcrowded. One-fifth of all Chinese housing units are without adequate plumbing systems.[18]

California has the largest Chinese population in the United States, which is 39 percent (170,400). Of this number of Chinese in California, about 24 percent (40,798) reside in Los Angeles County.[19] The number of Chinese who live in the city of Los Angeles is about 1 percent (27,345) of the total city population (2,816,061).[20]

In general, the Chinese are dispersed throughout the city and county of Los Angeles with no delineated community boundary of their own. The exception is New Chinatown, where the largest concentration of Chinese can be found.

Wen-Hui C. Chen in "Changing Socio-cultural Patterns of the Chinese Community in Los Angeles," indicated that most of the early Chinese who came to Los Angeles in 1850 were from San Francisco.[21] The history, characteristics, and problems of those Chinese were similar to the others who had settled down in many other cities. Chinatown was established for the purpose of meeting mutual needs and protection.[22]

---

[16]Ibid.

[17]Ibid.

[18]Ibid.

[19]U.S., Department of Commerce, Bureau of the Census, United States Census of Population: 1970, vol. 1, Characteristics of the Population, California

[20]Ibid.

[21]Wen-Hui Chung Chen, "Changing Socio-cultural Patterns of the Chinese Community in Los Angeles" (Ph.D. dissertation, University of Southern California, 1952), p. 75.

[22]Ibid., p. 73.

For the purpose of this study, two census tracts (197100 and 207100) located in the New Chinatown of Los Angeles were selected because of their high concentration of Chinese people and because their general characteristics were similar to those of the total Chinese population in the United States.

According to a report prepared by the Los Angeles City Community Analysis Bureau based on the 1970 Census data, about 65 percent of the population in these two census tracts were Chinese; Mexican-Americans were the next largest ethnic group comprising 27 percent of the population, and the remaining 8 percent were white and others (see Appendix A). The median income of the families in these two tracts was less than $8,000 annually. Automobile ownership rates were low--only 44 percent for the families who lived in the Downtown section (census tract 207100) and 75 percent for the families in the Elysian Park area (census tract 197100). About 17 percent of the families were in poverty in comparison to the city's average of about 10 percent. While 11 percent were on welfare, the unemployment rate was less than 5 percent.[23]

Commensurate with the low income characteristic of the area, home ownership was also reported to be low--only about 40 percent of the residents owned their homes. Most of the housing units were considered old since they were built before 1939. The lack of adequate plumbing facilities was another serious problem. The degree of overcrowing in these areas was high, with over 15 percent of the total housing units having 1.51 or more persons per room.[24]

The age distribution of the population was close to the city's average. About 30 percent of the population was under 18 years of age. The high school dropout rate of this population was comparable to the city's as a whole. However, the student reading achievement level was markedly low--the lowest 25 percent of the nation's average.[25]

Suicide and attempted suicide rates were very low in this area. The crime rate was also below that of the city average.

---

[23]City of Los Angeles, Bureau of Community Analysis, "The State of the City: A Cluster Analysis of Los Angeles," June 1974, p. 38.

[24] Ibid.

[25]Ibid., p. 41.

However, narcotic and juvenile delinquency arrests are rising, suggesting an escalation of crime.[26]

The health indicators reflected some positive trends. The death rates were low, and there were few births weighing less than five pounds. However, Chinese mothers tended to begin prenatal care a little later than most women in the city of Los Angeles. The proportion of women engaged in gainful employment was considerably higher than that of the city, although employment was primarily in blue collar occupations. Only 33 percent were employed in white collar jobs.[27]

In summary, these last two sections have presented a brief overview of the Chinese immigration experiences in this country, a national profile of the Chinese population which will be selected for this study. Several factors have been presented here. Early Chinese suffered bitter and depressing experiences immigrating to this country. They then had to struggle to settle in American communities. They also maintained unique Chinese cultural differences. These three facts might account for the feelings of many Chinese-Americans that although they are physically and geographically in America, they are psychologically and socially alienated. Whether or not these distinctive political, social, economic, and cultural background characteristics contribute to the conspicuously low rate of utilizing mental health services by Chinese-Americans is the concern and focus of this study.

Statement of the Problem

The utilization rate of community mental health services by Chinese-Americans has always been very low in Los Angeles. According to statistics published by the Los Angeles County Department of Health Services for the fiscal year of 1973-74, Chinese-American patients, including inpatient (0.38 percent) and outpatient (0.18 percent), served by the Los Angeles County Mental Health Services and other private contract facilities represented only 0.23 percent of the total patient population.[28] Revised 1970 Census data indicate that Chinese-Americans accounted

---

[26] Ibid.

[27] Ibid.

[28] County of Los Angeles, Department of Health Services, Discharges and Units of Services by Ethnic Origin: Fiscal Year 1973-74 (Los Angeles: Department of Health Services, Mental Health Research and Evaluation Division), Vol. III, No. 11, pp. 5-10.

for 0.64 percent of the population in this county.[29]   Therefore, the proportion of Chinese-Americans to the county population is approximately 2.8 times greater than their representation in mental health patient statistics. This striking underutilization by Chinese-Americans of mental health services is the highest for any of the identified racial or ethnic groups, excluding other Asians, in Los Angeles County.

A recent study of Chinese-Americans and other Asian college students also indicated a tendency for underutilization of mental health services at the University of California at Los Angeles.[30]   Another study conducted by Sue and McKinney in the State of Washington had similar findings. It also concluded that Chinese-Americans and other Asian-Americans show low utilization of mental health facilities but greater severity of mental symptoms when first seen at the community mental health clinics.[31]   A recent study has suggested that the rates of mental illness among Chinese-Americans and other Asian-Americans have been underestimated and that the resources for handling their mental health problems are inadequate.[32]

Unfortunately, these statistics often have the effect of reinforcing the commonly held stereotype of Chinese-Americans as a highly stable group, one that is economically well off, with tight family and kinship relationships, and a preference for "taking care of their own." The truth is that since 1930, the rate of state hospital commitments among Chinese-Americans has increased faster than that of the general population in California.[33]

[29]Greater Los Angeles Community Action Agency, Research and Evaluation Division, "Ethnicity of Los Angeles County Population, April, 1974." (mimeographed report).

[30]Stanley Sue and Derald W. Sue, "The Reflection of Cultural Conflict in the Psychological Problems of Chinese-Americans," paper presented at the First National Conference on Asian American Studies, Los Angeles, California, April 1971, p. 7.

[31]Stanley Sue and Herman McKinney, "Asian-American in the Community Mental Health System," American Journal of Orthopsychiatry 45 (January 1975): 111-118.

[32]Timothy Brown, Kenneth Stein, Katherine Huang, and Darrel Harris, "Mental Illness and the Role of Mental Health Facilities in Chinatown," in Asian-Americans: Psychological Perspectives, ed. S. Sue and N. Wagner (Palo Alto, Ca.: Science & Behavior Books, 1973), pp. 212-231.

[33]Bernard B. Berk and Lucie Cheng Hirata, "Mental Illness Among the Chinese: Myth or Reality?" Journal of Social Issues 29, No. 2 (1973), 149-166.

Another study found that the number of Chinese-American patients at a mental health center located in Chinatown increased about 200 percent over a two-year period after a bilingual program became available.[34]

There is a paucity of empirical knowledge regarding the mental health needs and problems of Chinese-Americans. Mental health services and programs are essentially a middle-class white activity.[35] While there have been conjectures, hypotheses, and in some cases studies which pointed toward various reasons--such as cultural and value system conflicts, language, inaccessibility of services, and the unresponsiveness of the system of services--for the underutilization of mental health services, there is a decided lack of empirical research on the mental health needs of the Chinese. As Kitano and Sue indicated, several factors have hindered the systematic and empirical studies of the Asian-Americans: (1) a general lack of interest in Asian-Americans, (2) difficulty in obtaining adequate samples, (3) problems of language, (4) problems of finding culturally unbiased research instruments, and (5) the hesitations of many Asians to act as subjects.[36]

As Finestone indicated, effective and efficient mental health services demand a familiarity with and an understanding of distinct ethnic groups' mental health needs--their aspirations as well as their fears and concerns.[37] Too often, the assessment of needs are drawn from theories or from indirect or impressionistic studies. In this study, the focus was on potential and perhaps even actual mental health patients. It asked what Chinese-Americans consider to be mental illness, how they cope with mental illness when it strikes, what knowledge they have of services, what their attitudes toward existing services are, and their perceptions of barriers to receiving needed services.

---

[34] Herbert K. Hatanaka, Bill Y. Watanabe, and Shin 'ya Ono, "The Utilization of Mental Health Services by Asian Americans in Los Angeles Area," Proceedings of Service Delivery in Pan Asian Communities, ed. Wesley H. Ishikawa and Nikki Hayashi Archer (San Diego: Pacific Asian Coalition Mental Health Training Center, 1975), p. 37.

[35] Bernard M. Kramer, "Racism and Mental Health as a Field of Thought and Action," in Racism and Mental Health (Pittsburgh: University of Pittsburgh Press, 1973), p. 3.

[36] Harry Kitano and Stanley Sue, "The Model Minorities," Journal of Social Issues 29, No. 2 (1973): 4.

[37] Samuel Finestone, Community Mental Health Services in New York City (New York: Center for New York City Affairs, 1973), pp. 74-75.

Survey of the Literature

A review of the pertinent literature indicated that there were two common explanations for the underutilization of community mental health services by Chinese-Americans. The first notion suggests that definitions of what mental illness is and what kinds of treatment are appropriate are determined by a group's cultural orientation. The second notion suggests that the utilization of community mental health services is determined by the community's knowledge of mental health resources, attitudes about the quality and appropriateness of such services, and perceptions of barriers to the receipt of services. These two notions led to the formulation of the conceptual framework (Figure 1) which guided the direction and sequence of this study.

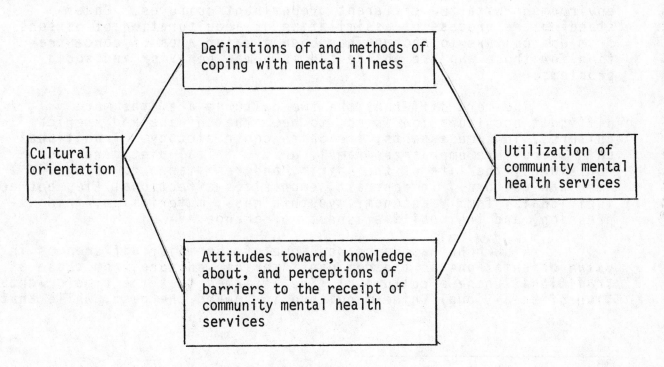

Figure 1. Conceptual Framework

Cultural Orientation
and Chinese-Americans

Culture plays an important role in the socialization process of all people. Culture is a part of each human being, and every phase of a person's life and thought mirrors that culture. Attitudes, values, personality, behavior and knowledge are all reflections of the individual's cultural heritage and orientation.[38]

As Fenlanson stated, every culture is of paramount importance to its possessor; one who functions in a culture is part of it, and every aspect of his action and thought reflect that culture.[39] In order to understand an individual's attitude or actions, it is necessary to see his behavior in terms of his cultural orientation. An individual's behavior becomes more complex and less well understood when he has grown up in environment with two different predominant cultures. Understanding the process of assimilation or acculturation of persons from one culture to another has been a major area of concentration for those who are interested in human behavior and social problems.

The more different the two cultures are, the more difficult acculturation is apt to be. The Chinese and American cultures, in some aspects, are quite contradictory. Traditional Chinese culture emphasizes family unity, filial piety, respect for elders, the life of the spirit, and resistance to change. American cultural, in contrast, emphasizes affectional ties between individuals, family autonomy, youthfulness, materialism, free expression, and the positive aspects of change.[40]

Kluckhohn has described some of the major differences in value orientations of the dominant American culture from those of traditional Chinese culture.[41] She affirmed that the time orientation of traditional Chinese culture is toward the past, while that

---

[38] *The Columbia Encyclopedia* (New York: Columbia University Press, 1962), p. 521.

[39] Anne T. Fenlanson, *Essentials in Interviewing* (New York: Harper and Row, Publishers, 1962), pp. 12-36.

[40] Peter W. Chen, "Cultural Conflict and Mental Illness: A Case Study of a Mentally Ill Chinese-American Patient" (MSW thesis, California State University at Fresno, 1968), p. 3.

[41] Florence Rochwood Kluckhohn, "Family Diagnosis. I. Variations in the Basic Values of Family System," *Social Casework* 39 (February-March 1958): 66-69.

of the dominant American culture is toward the future. The primary relational orientation of the Chinese people is toward lineal ties; the American people, on the other hand, tend to be individualistic. The essential man-nature orientation of the traditional Chinese culture stresses harmony with nature, while that of the dominant American culture is concerned with mastery over nature. The activity orientation of the Chinese culture emphasizes the individual as he is, with emphasis also on his development; the activity orientation of the American culture places the emphasis on doing, accomplishing, and succeeding.

Betty Sung has pointed out that the cultural bridge between China and America is much wider than that between America and the nations of Europe. In speech, attitude, religion, philosophy, and outlook, Chinese ways are vastly different and identifiable physical differences set the two groups apart.[42]

The Chinese-Americans, no matter whether they were foreign born or native born, are constantly confronted with Western cultural values and customs outside of their immediate family and cultural group. They must learn two cultures and acquire two identities, each vastly different from the other. A person who possesses a strong identification with his native culture is especially likely to have difficulty performing and adjusting adequately to the new culture. Problems of status identification became accentuated and conflicts within the family arise.[43]

Throughout the years, Asian immigrants, beginning with the Chinese, have experienced racial prejudice and discrimination. Even federal and state laws were passed to harass and discriminate against the Chinese; these laws denied them citizenships, prohibited the ownership of land, etc.[44] Social and political conditions have changed somewhat and there has been less discrimination against the Chinese in recent years. More recent government policies have tended to promote and support the "melting pot policy" which calls for minority groups, including the Chinese,

---

[42] Betty Lee Sung, Mountain of Gold (New York: The Macmillan Co., 1967), p. 133.

[43] Stanley L. Fond, "Identity Conflicts of Chinese Adolescents in San Francisco," in Minority Group Adolescents in the United States, ed. E. Brody (Baltimore: Williams & Wilkins, 1968); and B. Wright, "Social Aspects of Change in the Chinese Family Pattern in Hong Kong," Journal of Social Psychology 63 (1964): 31-39.

[44] Roger Daniels, Racism in California (New York: The Macmillan Co., 1972), pp. 58-66.

to adopt the customs and language of the dominant society.[45]
Whether the Chinese are willing to be assimilated or whether
the white majority is ready to facilitate this remains a question.

One of the most comprehensive portrayals of Chinese-
Americans and their cultural orientations is Stanley Sue and
Derald Sue's study, "Chinese-American Personality and Mental
Health."[46] They suggest that there are three major types of
adaptations that the Chinese can develop in the process of
acculturation or assimilation (Figure 2).

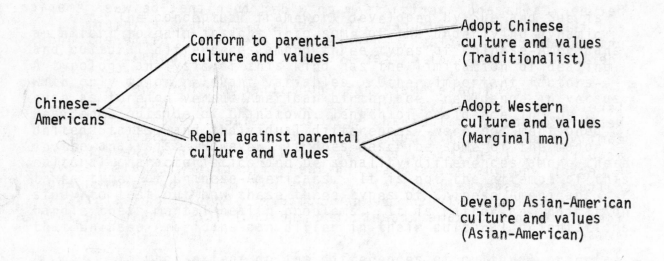

Figure 2. Adaptation Patterns of Chinese-Americans

The first type is the Traditionalist who remains com-
mitted to a traditional Chinese cultural orientation. Emphasis
is placed on obtaining a good education, on being obedient to
parents, and in giving the family a good name. "Bad" behavior--
such as, anti-social or criminal behavior, disobedience, low

_____

[45]Stuart Creighton Miller, The Unwelcome Immigrant (Berkeley: University
of California Press, 1969), pp. 190-192.

[46]Stanley Sue and Derald W. Sue, "Chinese-American Personality and Mental
Health," in Asian-Americans: Psychological Perspectives, ed. S. Sue and
N. Wagner (Palo Alto, Ca.: Science and Behavior Book, Inc., 1973),
pp. 111-124.

achievement, or even psychopathology--is believed to bring shame on the entire family. The Traditionalist, alone, bears the responsibility for his failure, for he cannot blame his parents nor the society. Since role expectations in the Chinese family are well defined and structured, he may find it difficult to interact with Caucasians, who are often behaving under different expectations. For example, Caucasian patterns of relating tend to stress assertive and spontaneous behaviors. The Chinese patterns of deference and reserve are at odds with these values.[47] Whenever the Traditionalist encounters interpersonal conflicts or psychological problems, he is not likely to seek psychotherapy or mental health services. As Sue and Sue indicated, the Traditionalist does not understand psychotherapy and feels great shame about admitting to psychological problems.[48] Furthermore, the structure, sanctions, and internal operations of the traditional Chinese family tend to deny symptoms and prevent a mentally ill member from receiving mental health services.

The second type of Chinese is the Marginal person who exists between the margin of two cultures and suffers from an identity crisis. He attempts to assimilate and acculturate into the American society. In attempts to resolve his cultural or value conflicts, he may reject traditional Chinese ways by becoming over-Americanized. Hostility toward and denial of his Chinese cultural orientation may cause him to turn his hostility inward and to develop a form of "racial self-hatred."[49] For instance, he may hate himself for possessing "Chinese" characteristics, such as shortness of height, round-flat nose, narrow eyes, etc. He may also hate himself for hating himself. Whenever the Marginal man encounters problems or conflicts, he may view psychotherapy or mental health services more favorably than other groups of Chinese because of his attempts to assimilate to the American culture.[50]

The third type of Chinese-American is the Asian-American who tries to formulate a new identity by integrating his Chinese cultural orientation with present American conditions. For example, he feels that complete obedience to traditional Chinese culture limits his self growth. Self-pride cannot be attained if his behaviors are completely determined by his parents or by society. Parental emphasis on high achievement is too materialistic for the Asian-American who is trying to find meaning and

---

[47] Sue and Sue, "Chinese Personality and Mental Health," pp. 113-114.

[48] Ibid., p. 119.

[49] Ibid., pp. 115-116.

[50] Gorden Allport, The Nature of Prejudice (New York: Doubleday and Co., 1958), pp. 147-148.

self-identity. In addition, he is more sensitive to negative forces in society which have shaped his identity and have too often been left unchallenged. Problems such as poverty, unemployment, individual and institutional racism, and mental illness are of primary concern to him. He believes that more than anything else, society is to blame for his present dilemma and that it must be changed. As a consequence, the Asian-American may become extremely militant in fighting for civil rights, self-pride, and power. Whenever the Asian-American encounters interpersonal or psychological problems he is not likely to utilize mental health services because he equates such treatment with the status quo and is openly suspicious of this type of activity.[51]

The conceptual framework developed by Sue and Sue is an effort to gain insight into some of the underlying dynamic and cultural differences among three types of Chinese-Americans. A typology analysis of this kind has the limitation of dealing with only major relevant variables. Other important factors-- such as foreign versus American birthplace, residence in versus residence outside of Chinatown, length of residence in the United States, and individual differences--were not mentioned in the analysis. However, it does describe some of the major cultural characteristics and personality differences among these three types of Chinese-Americans. It is not the attempt of this study to test out how these three types of Chinese Americans handle their mental health problems. It is rather an indication that Chinese-Americans can differ in their cultural orientations.

To what extent do the differences of cultural orientation affect an individual's definitions of mental illness or whether he utilizes mental health services when they are needed? How do the demographic characteristics; such as place of birth, length of stay in the United States, years of education in the United States, etc. affect individual's cultural orientation? These questions have never been empirically examined for Chinese-Americans, and are the major concern of this study.

Definitions of and Methods
of Coping with Mental Illness

This study is based on the belief that various ethnic groups manifest different definitions of and utilize different methods of coping with mental illness. In other words, the beliefs among members of an ethnic group as to what constitutes

---

[51] Sue and Sue, "Chinese Personality and Mental Health," p. 116.

mental illness and its appropriate treatment are formed and supported by generally held cultural attitudes.[52] For instance, a member of a particular society who perceives himself as being mentally ill may expect psychotherapy as the proper treatment. For this to occur, his society would have to recognize the existence of such mental incapacity and sanction psychotherapy as appropriate and effective treatment. However, in another society and/or cultural system, the same symptoms or illness might be regarded as signs of demoniacal possession which is to be treated by exorcism.[53]

How and in what terms people value health and what their beliefs are about methods of preserving health, are important issues in mental health practice. In many parts of the world, the mentally ill suffer and die not only due to a lack of knowledge and treatment but also because of their attitudes toward and beliefs about mental illness and services. An analogous example can be drawn from the sect of Jehovah's Witnesses, which does not believe in blood transfusions.[54]

There have been numerous studies of public attitudes toward the mentally ill in the United States. One example is Shirley Star's survey of attitudes toward mental illness, conducted by the National Opinion Research Center in the early 1950s. She found significant correlations between the levels of socioeconomic status and the perceptions of and attitudes toward mental illness.[55] Asking 3,500 respondents about six descriptions of mentally ill persons, Star found that 17 percent of the sample did not identify any of them as mentally ill. Another 28 percent limited their concept of mental illness to the paranoid schizophrenic.

Elaine and John Cumming, who adopted Star's instruments, used the same six vignettes in a Canadian town and found that the majority of their respondents failed to recognize mental illness; they did not consider certain serious symptoms to

---

[52] Talcott Parsons, "Illness and Role of the Physician: A Sociological Perspectives," American Journal of Orthopsychiatry 21 (1951): 452-460; and Sebastian DeGrazia, Errors of Psychotherapy (New York: Doubleday & Co., 1952).

[53] Jerome D. Frank, "The Dynamics of the Psychotherapeutic Relationship," in Mental Illness and Social Processes, ed. Thomas J. Scheff (New York: Harper & Row Publishers, 1967), p. 170.

[54] Fredrick C. Redlich and Daniel X. Freedman, The Theory and Practice of Psychiatry (New York: Basic Books, Inc., 1966), p. 800.

[55] Shirley A. Star, "The Public's Ideas about Mental Illness," paper presented at the meeting of the National Association of Mental Health, Indianapolis, Indiana, 5 November, 1955.

indicate disturbed behavior, even when they were clinically grave. Instead, they would make comments such as: "It's just a quirk, it's nothing serious."[56]

On the other hand, contradictory findings were reported by Lemkau and Crocetti who used three of Star's case vignettes in Baltimore and found that 91 percent of their sample identified the paranoid as mentally ill, and 62 percent saw the alcoholic as mentally ill.[57] Their findings also reflected the notion that people of low socioeconomic status, both Black and White, were relatively well prepared to identify and understand mental illness.

Dohrenwend, Bernard, and Kolb also applied Star's six case abstracts to "leaders in an urban area" and found that "all saw mental illness in the description of the paranoid; 72 percent saw it correctly in the example of simple schizophrenia; 63 percent in the alcoholic; about 50 percent in the anxiety neurosis and in the juvenile character disorder; and 40 percent in the compulsivephobic."[58]

Marvin Karno and Robert Edgerton studied the perception of mental illness in East Los Angeles and found that the under-utilization of community mental health services by Mexican-Americans was not due to cultural ethnocentrism but rather the problem of communication--the inability to speak English. The results of their study further indicated that Mexican-Americans' perceptions of mental illness were not different from those of whites.[59]

Although the findings of these various studies were somewhat inconsistent, they do indicate that there are differences in perceptions of mental illness among people with different social, economical, and cultural backgrounds.

---

[56]Elaine Cumming and John Cumming, "Affective Symbolism, Social Norms, and Mental Illness," Journal of Psychiatry 19 (February 1956): 77-85.

[57]Paul V. Lemkau and Guido M. Crocetti, "An Urban Population's Opinion and Knowledge about Mental Illness," The American Journal of Psychiatry 118 (1962): 694.

[58]Bruce P. Dohrenwend, Viola W. Bernard, and Lawrence C. Kolb, "The Orientation of Leaders in an Urban Area Toward Problems of Mental Illness," The American Journal of Psychiatry 118 (1962): 683-691.

[59]Marvin Karno and Robert B. Edgerton, "Perception of Mental Illness in a Mexican-American Community," The Archives of General Psychiatry 20 (February 1969): 233-238.

Margaret Clark's study of the health needs and health behavioral patterns of Mexican-Americans in San Jose found that Mexican-Americans still believed in their traditional folk medicine in diagnosing and treating their sickness and health problems. The rejection of modern approaches to the treatment of illness was thought to be due to a number of direct and indirect reasons: partial or spatial segregation of the community, language difficulties, fear of discrimination or insult by whites, strong loyalties to the family and the neighborhood group, the desire to avoid conflict with group members, a fear of shame or ridicule for departure from cultural traditions, the dream of many older folk of someday returning to Mexico, and the fear and suspicion of the unknown.[60]

While there have been ample studies of perceptions, attitudes, and beliefs toward mental illness and health problems among various groups, there is a decided lack of investigation of the Chinese population. Hopefully, this study will help in the development of understanding of the underutilization of mental health services by Chinese-Americans. It was this phenomenon which generated the interest for such an investigation.

Utilization of Community Mental
Health Services: Attitudes,
Knowledge, and Perceptions of
Barriers

This section discusses the idea that the lack of information and knowledge about mental health resources may result in underutilization of existing community mental health facilities and services. Furthermore, various cultural values, attitudes, and taboos may be factors which enter into whether Chinese-Americans avoid knowing or deny the existence of such resources.

As Alfred Kahn indicated, there are many difficulties involved in the delivery of social services; some of these are the availability and accessibility of services, a shortage of qualified manpower, and stigmatization of the users.[61] Studies in the use of health services have shown that the utilization of health services is highly related to such factors as the

---

[60]Margaret Clark, Health in the Mexican-American Culture (Berkeley: University of California Press, Ltd., 1970), p. 238.

[61]Alfred J. Kahn, Studies in Social Policy and Planning (New York: Russell Sage Foundation, 1969), pp. 245-259.

accessibility of the facilities, the knowledge about the services on the part of potential users, and the users' attitude toward the services.[62]

The mentally ill person is frequently viewed by the general public as deviant and therefore to be avoided. Sarbin and Mancuso studied public attitudes toward mental illness and found that the illness or medical model as a formula for understanding and controlling deviant behavior had not been widely accepted by the public. The public seemed to be more tolerant of deviant behavior when it was not labeled as mental illness.[63] Because of certain types of stigma attached to persons with mental illness symptoms, individuals--especially those from social or cultural groups which label such behavior as taboo-- almost always try to keep these conditions hidden or avoid seeking professional help.

Giordano concluded in his study, Ethnicity and Mental Health, that because of the stigma attached to mental illness, even whites had negative feelings about using mental health services. Blacks and other ethnic minority groups, faced with many feelings of powerlessness and alienation, failed to even perceive their mental health needs. As a partial solution, he suggested that mental health professionals work harder to convey respect for the ethnic life-style, self-identification, and community structure of minority groups.[64]

Aside from these social and cultural aspects, there are other factors that have tended to discourage the poor and ethnic minorities from using mental health services. A number of studies have addressed the questions of the relative acceptability of low and high socioeconomic class patients for therapy. For

---

[62]Lawrence Padell, "Studies in the Use of Health Services by Families on Welfare: Utilization of Preventive Health Services," The Center for Study of Urban Problems, New York City, 1969, pp. 21-38; and Roger M. Ballislilla, "Utilization of Preventive-Diagnostic Services Among Late Adulthood Persons," Center for Housing and Environmental Studies, Cornell University, New York, February 1969.

[63]T. R. Sarbin and J. C. Mancuso, "Failure of a Moral Enterprise: Attitudes of the Public Toward Mental Illness," Journal of Counseling and Clinical Psychology 35, No. 2 (1970), 159-173.

[64]J. Giordano, Ethnicity and Mental Health: Research and Recommendations

20

example, Brill and Storrow indicated that members of the lower socioeconomic classes were less apt to be accepted for treatment than members of the upper socioeconomic classes.[65] Harrison and his colleagues reported a similar finding in their study of a child guidance clinic and concluded that the children of professional and executive parents received psychotherapy much more frequently than children of lower status groups.[66] Yamamoto and Goin compared employed and unemployed patients and found that approximately one-fourth of the employed applicants were given individual therapy, whereas only about one in thirty of the chronically unemployed applicants were offered such therapy.[67] In another study, Lief and his associates reported findings consistent with the above studies and indicated that, at the clinic studied, 62 percent of the patients accepted for treatment were college graduates, whereas only 18 percent of those denied had completed college.[68]

The relationships between socioeconomic status of patients and therapists have also been explored through research. For instance, at a children's clinic, Baker and Wagner found that upper-class patients tended to be assigned to psychiatrists or psychiatric residents, whereas lower-class patients were usually assigned to social workers and psychologists.[69] Yamamoto and his associates found that the lower a therapist's ethnocentricity score, the longer he tended to see Black as compared to Caucasian patients.[70] In another study, Hasse found that patients of lower socioeconomic status were diagnosed as more

---

[65]N. Brill and N. Storrow, "Social Class and Psychiatric Treatment," The Archives of General Psychiatry 3 (1960): 340-344.

[66]S. Harrison, et al., "Social Class and Mental Illness in Children: Choice of Treatment," The Archives of General Psychiatry 13 (1965): 411-416.

[67]J. Yamamoto and M. Goin, "Social Class Factors Relevant for Psychiatric Treatment," Journal of Nervous and Mental Disease 142 (1966): 332-339.

[68]H. Lief, et al., "Low Dropout Rate in a Psychiatric Clinic Special Reference to Psychotherapy and Social Class," The Archives of General Psychiatry 5 (1961): 200-211.

[69]J. Baker and N. Wagner, "Social Class and Treatment in a Child Psychiatry Clinic," The Archives of General Psychiatry 14 (1966): 129-133.

[70]Joseph Yamamoto, et al., "Racial Factors in Patient Selection," Journal of American Psychiatry 124 (1967): 630-637.

disturbed and received poorer prognoses than did upper-class patients.[71]

Social work researchers have also studied the importance to treatment of racial differences between social worker and client. Fibush, Simmons, Rosen and Frank, Curry, Bloch, and Fischer and Miller all found that race and social class have strong effect on social workers' clinical judgments: lower social class clients were seen more negatively than upper class clients and the factor of race became an important variable in the treatment process when the caseworker and the client were members of different racial groups.[72] Roberts, however, found no significant relationship between client's social class and caseworkers' clinical judgments of child abuse cases.[73]

The findings of these various studies suggest that people of lower socioeconomic status and those who are members of ethnic minority groups face more obstacles than the advantaged in seeking mental health services. The following are some studies and literature related to attitudes, knowledge, and awareness levels of the Chinese in relation to their utilization of existing services and/or facilities.

Brown and his associates found support for the hypothesis that the Chinese patients were unfamiliar with and/or reluctant to use mental health facilities.[74] They also found evidence of more pronounced psychiatric disturbance among Chinese in-patients than among Caucasians. This led to the conclusion that Chinese

---

[71] W. Hasse, "Research Diagnosis, Socioeconomic Class and Examiner Bias," (Doctoral dissertation, New York University, 1956).

[72] E. Fibush, "The White Worker and the Negro Client," Social Casework 46 (1965): 271-277; L. Simmons, "Crow Jim: Implications for Social Work," Social Work 8 (1963): 24-30; H. Rosen and J. Frank, "Negroes in Psychotherapy," in Mental Health of the Poor, ed. F. Riessman et al. (New York: Free Press, 1964), pp. 393-399; A. Curry, "The Negro Worker and the White Client," Social Casework 45 (1964): 131-136; J. Bloch, "The White Worker and the Negro Client in Psychotherapy," Social Work 13 (1968): 36-42; Joel Fischer and Henry Miller, "The Effect of Client Race and Social Class on Clinical Judgments," Clinical Social Work Journal 1, No. 2 (1973): 100-109.

[73] Robert W. Roberts, "A Study of Social Workers' Judgments of Child Abuse" (DSW dissertation, Columbia University, 1970), pp. 188-198.

[74] Brown, "Mental Health Facilities in Chinatown," p. 223.

families will use psychiatric hospitalization only as a last resort, such as in the case of severe incapacitation of the head of the household.[75] The study concluded with a recommendation for increased outreach efforts to facilitate early and preventive treatment of Chinese patients.

Another survey regarding the utilization of social services by Asians was conducted in Sacramento, California. The findings indicated that among the Asian-American groups, the Chinese were the most in need of social services but the least likely to take advantage of them.[76] Language barriers and limited knowledge about sources of information appeared to be the major reasons for the low utilization of social services by the Chinese.

Chen's study of the Chinese community in Los Angeles revealed that many Chinese clients did not seek out psychiatric help simply because they did not consider "emotional support" as a form of help to them. In addition, she asserted that while the "silent" Chinese do have a myriad of problems, their strong sense of shame and pride have precluded and hindered their use of community programs and services.[77]

A study of Mandarin-speaking aged Chinese in the Los Angeles area conducted by Frances Wu concluded that the sample group had numerous unmet social and health needs. The shortage of service facilities, lack of information regarding sources, language barrier, and limited transportation were the major obstacles which prevented the aged Chinese from obtaining help.[78] Whether the lack of information accompanied by language and attitude barriers are also evident in the general Chinatown resident population remains to be investigated.

---

[75]Ibid.

[76]Ivy Lee, "A Profile of Asians in Sacramento," U.S. Department of Health, Education, and Welfare Grant No. IROIMH 21086-01, September 30, 1973. (Mimeographed report.)

[77]Pei-Ngor Chen, "The Chinese Community in Los Angeles," Social Work 15 (December 1970): 591-598.

[78]Frances Yu-Ching Wu, "Mandarin-Speaking Aged Chinese in Los Angeles Area: Needs and Services" (DSW dissertation, University of Southern California, 1974).

CHAPTER II

RESEARCH QUESTIONS, DESIGN, AND METHODOLOGY

This chapter provides a description of the research questions, research design, and methodology used in this study. The detailed description includes the following: the purpose of the study, the research questions, underlying assumptions upon which the study was based, definitions of major terms, the research design, selection of the sample, and data collection and data analysis.

Purpose of the Study

The purpose of this study was to examine Chinese-Americans' definitions of and methods for coping with mental illness as well as attitudes toward, knowledge about, and perceptions of barriers to receiving mental health services. This study also explored the relationships between Chinese-Americans' cultural orientations and their mental health judgments. Hopefully, the results of this study will provide some insights and familiarity about the perceived attitudes, beliefs, knowledge, and needs among this Chinese group that exhibits a conspicuously low rate of using community mental health services in Los Angeles County. In addition to expanding the knowledge of mental health problems of Chinese-Americans, the results of this study also have a potential significance for mental health practice, program, and policy development. This study also offers a base for reassessment of current mental health programs and such other arrangements as treatment modalities, location of facilities, and composition of treatment staff in programs and services in areas having concentrations of Chinese-Americans. Finally, to the social work profession, this study will hopefully be a contribution to an expanding body of knowledge for improving services to ethnic minorities in general.

Research Questions

The specific research questions which were formulated to guide the investigation are the following:

1. How do Chinese-Americans perceive and cope with mental illness? Are their perceptions and methods of coping with mental illness different from other ethnic groups?

2. To what extent do Chinese-Americans accept the Western concept of mental illness and its treatment?

3. What are Chinese-Americans' attitudes toward, knowledge about, and perceptions of barriers to receiving mental health services?

4. Are variations in the traditional Chinese cultural orientation related to Chinese-Americans' mental health judgments? If so, are these relationships affected by selected personal characteristics?

Assumptions

A review of the literature on concepts of mental illness and the underlying dynamics of cultural attitudes toward mental health service utilization led to the following assumptions:

1. Mental health problems are normally distributed in the population. In other words, Chinese-Americans should experience as many mental health problems as other ethnic groups do, despite their differences in cultural backgrounds and orientation.

2. The perceptions, attitudes, and identified needs of community residents or potential consumers of community mental health services are valid and important in program or policy formulation in spite of their ethnocentric biases.

3. Although there are geographical and generation differences between American-born Chinese and those who recently immigrated here, they are considered as a homogeneous group in this study. This assumption is necessary because the data obtained in this survey did not permit an empirical testing of the assumption.

4. The majority of the people who utilize the community mental health services are in the range of low to middle socio-economic status. The Census data document that most residents of

New Chinatown are of the socioeconomic classes designated as target populations by community mental health programs. Thus, it is assumed that the opinions of Chinese residents in New Chinatown can be used as one basis for making policy and program decisions in the field of mental health.

Definitions of Major Terms

This study utilizes a number of terms, some of which may not be familiar to the reader. For the purpose of providing some clarity in understanding the content of this study, these terms are defined as the following:

Chinese-Americans. The term "Chinese-Americans" shall be used to refer to persons of Chinese ancestry who were born and reared in the United States as well as those who immigrated here.

Community mental health services. In November 1957, California was one of the few states which had adopted a community mental health program. This shifted the responsibility of providing mental health services and treatment of mentally ill persons from the state government to county governments and was based on the assumption that a locally planned, developed, and administered mental health program might best meet the community needs as well as have a better chance of obtaining local support. The county sponsored community mental health programs, known as the Short-Doyle programs, have 75 percent or 90 percent state funding and 25 percent or 10 percent local funding. These programs generally consist of outpatient services, inpatient services, partial hospitalization services, emergency services, rehabilitation services, and precare and aftercare services in the community. It also makes mandatory provisions for training, research, and evaluation.[1]

In the 1960s, federally funded nonprofit community mental health centers were established. In many instances, they received both federal construction and staffing funds in order to meet the mental health needs of a defined population residing within a catchment area. In 1970, these nonprofit community mental health centers were encouraged to establish innovative treatment services with government matching funds. The purpose was to broaden and complement services already offered by the

---

[1] State of California, California Mental Health Services Act (Sacramento: Department of Health, 1974).

local community mental health programs. These so called "contracted" Short-Doyle programs, like the Resthaven Community Mental Health Center, the Gateways Community Mental Health Center, etc., were set up to follow this system of providing mental health services.

Mental illness. Mental illness refers to a range of disorders, related to a still unclear combination of physiological, psychological, emotional, and behavioral disabilities. Many mental disorders are accompanied by distortions of personality function and by distortions of the affected persons' social relationships.[2]

Western concepts of mental illness and its treatment. The term "Western" is used here to differentiate it from the Eastern or Chinese. To be more specific, it refers to concepts that are accepted by the general Americans. A Likert-type scale containing seven five-point items was constructed to operationalize Western concepts of mental illness and its treatment. Four items were related to the cause of mental illness; including statements such as: mental illness is inherited, mental illness is brought on as punishment for sins, mental illness arises from tensions and trouble in the family, and mental illness arises from lack of willpower. The other three items were related to the treatment methods for mental illness; including statements such as: Chinese medicine is effective in treating mental illness, counseling and psychotherapy is effective treatment, and a mentally ill person can recover faster if he is with his family. Each item was given a score of from one to five, with the higher score representing attitudes that were most accepting Western concepts of mental illness and its treatment. Because each item was a five-point scale, the total possible score of the scale ranged from 7 to 35. The actual range of scores on this acceptance scale was from 13 to 29, however. The median score of 21 was used to divide the respondents into two groups. Those respondents with a total score of 21 or higher were considered to have more accepting attitudes toward Western concepts of mental illness and its treatment. Those respondents with scores below 21 were considered to have less accepting attitudes toward Western concepts of mental illness and its treatment.

Chinese cultural orientation. This term was defined by using a 15-item Likert-type scale. The major concepts involved in this scale are related to the respondents' identity and inclination toward traditional Chinese culture. For instance,

---

[2]National Association of Social Workers, Encyclopedia of Social Work (New York: NASW, 1965), p. 486.

items were about respondents' cultural practices such as Chinese
festival celebration, Chinese language ability, eating Chinese
meals, reading Chinese newspapers, having Chinese friends, shopping in Chinatown, feeling secure in Chinatown, special efforts
to send children to Chinese language school, and ways of resolv-
ing emotional or living problems within the family. (For more
detail, refer to Part IV of Appendix B.)

        Since each item was rated on a five-point scale, the
total possible score of this Chinese cultural orientation scale
ranged from 15 to 75. The actual range of scores was from 18 to
57 on this cultural orientation scale. The median score of 36
was used to divide the respondents into two groups, those with
more traditional and those with less traditional Chinese cultural
orientations.

        Utilization and underutilization of community mental
health services. Utilization refers to the use of existing
community mental health services provided by the Los Angeles
County Department of Health Services as well as the contracted
Short-Doyle mental health facilities. The term "underutilization"
is used in this study when an ethnic group's proportion in mental
health admission statistics is lower than its representation in
the county-wide population. This is based on the assumption that
the incidence of mental illness is the same throughout the population.

The Research Design

        The purpose of this study was to gain familiarity with
and an understanding of Chinese-Americans' cultural orientation
in relation to their definition of mental illness and their attitudes toward and knowledge about mental health services, and
their perceptions of barriers to receiving mental health services.
A review of literature indicated that there was only limited
knowledge available and that it was not realistic to advance
precise hypotheses. Instead, a descriptive and exploratory type
of study seemed most appropriate. In this study, the first step
was the examination and description of Chinese-Americans' definitions of and methods of coping with mental illness. The second
step was the examination and description of Chinese-Americans'
attitudes toward, knowledge about, and perceptions of barriers
to receiving mental health services. The third step was the
identification of the cultural orientation of the respondents
and an exploration of the relationships of cultural orientation
with the perceptions, attitudes, and knowledge of mental health
services, and barriers to receiving mental health services.

Because Chinese-Americans were the focus of this study, the most feasible design was to develop a sampling plan within a small homogeneous community of high Chinese concentration.

Selection of the Sample

The research design required an adequate sample of Chinese-Americans where general characteristics and social indicators of the population at large in a specified geographical area could be obtained. Based on the United States Census of 1970, two census tracts (197000 and 207100) located in New Chinatown of Los Angeles were selected as the sampling frame because of their high concentration of Chinese residents (see Appendix A). Another rationale for this selection was that the majority of people who utilize community mental health services come from the low socioeconomic group. The Chinese who lived in these two census tracts were in this low socioeconomic level.

A sample of one hundred Chinese adults was randomly selected from these two census tracts. Because there was no way to establish or obtain a sampling frame of all Chinese residents in these two census tracts, the city block maps were used as an alternative method. This method required the resolution of three problems: (1) some residents of ethnic origins other than Chinese would be accidentally selected in this process, (2) some of the addresses shown on the city block maps might not have a household or be a dwelling, and (3) some of the selected residents might refuse to be interviewed for this study. The solution used was the random selection of 150 addresses, so that one hundred participants would be obtained.

The field visits and interviews were conducted by six experienced and qualified researchers and assistants between July and October of 1975. Of the 150 addresses selected in this study, one hundred were accepted as the participants for the study, 13 were non-Chinese, 17 refused to participate, 14 were empty lots, and 6 more were unused. In other words, only 17 out of 117 or 14.5 percent of the Chinese did not want to participate in this study. The apparently low rejection rate for a field study could be attributed to the composition of the research teams, each of which had both male and female Chinese interviewers with full dialect coverages (Mandarin, Cantonese, Taishanese, and English) going out on each interview.

A procedure was further developed to assure the randomization of the total sample selected. If there was more than one unit or household at the same address, the representative of that sample would be selected through another process of randomization.

The first adult seen by the research team was expected to be the representative of that particular sample household. It was hoped that these procedures of sample selection increased the likelihood of a sample which is representative of the population of the households of the area.

Source of Data

The two major sources of data for this study were: (1) pertinent literature, documents, and previous studies; and (2) actual field interviews.

Review of the pertinent literature and documents enabled the researcher to gain some insights and identify concepts relating to the study. Review of the literature also facilitated a more precise formulation of the research questions, the research design, the focus of the study, and framework for analysis. Related previous studies provided further conceptual, methodological, and comparative clues in the conduct of the investigation and data analysis.

The actual field interviews and household survey gave firsthand information and data needed for this study. The one hundred randomly selected participants served as representatives or informants of the population under study, because limitations of time, manpower, and money prevented a census of all Chinese residents in New Chinatown of Los Angeles.

Research Instrument

Data for this survey study were obtained by the use of an interview schedule consisting of both "fixed-alternative" and "open-ended" questions. This research instrument, for conceptual as well as analytic purposes, was divided into five major parts.

The first part of the instrument was adopted from the instruments developed by Dr. Shirley Star at the National Opinion Research Center. Star's instruments consist of six examples of common mental illness (paranoid schizophrenia, simple schizophrenia, chronic anxiety neurosis, obsessive compulsive phobic neurosis, alcoholism, and a childhood behavior disorder). It has been used, in part or in whole, in over a dozen research projects in such areas as Baltimore, Chicago, New York, rural Canada, and East Los Angeles. It has also been used with a variety of social class and ethnic subcultural groups with good results.

To economize on interviewing time, only four of the six mental case examples in the Star's instruments were used in this study. To make these vignettes realistic for the population under study, the persons described were given common Chinese names. In all other aspects, the case materials were unchanged. The cases used were the examples of paranoid schizophrenia, simple schizophrenia, obsessive compulsive phobic neurosis, and childhood behavior disorder (see Appendix B). This portion of the instrument was used to obtain data about respondents' perceptions of mental illness and their methods of coping with these four common types of mental patients. The data obtained from this part of the instrument enabled comparisons to be made with some of the studies by other researchers in order to compare how Chinese-Americans differed from other cultural or ethnic groups in their perceptions of and methods of coping with mental illness.

The second part of the instrument consisted of a ten-item Likert-type scale. The objective of this part of the instrument was to gather data about the respondents' relative acceptance of the Western concept of mental illness and its treatment (see Appendix B). Of the ten items, only seven were retained to form the acceptance scale following the process of item analysis.[3] Three items were eliminated because an item analysis revealed that they lacked the power to discriminate between those whose scores placed them in the low and high quartiles (see Appendix C). The acceptance scale was used as one dependent variable in the study.

The third part of the instrument consisted of questions relative to respondents' attitudes about, knowledge of, and perceptions of barriers to receiving community mental health services (see Appendix B). All of these items were used as dependent variables in the study.

The fourth part of the instrument of this study was a 16-item Likert-type scale that assessed respondents' commitment to a traditional Chinese cultural orientation. Only one

---

[3]For a discussion on construction of Likert-type scales and procedure of item analysis, see Clarie Selltiz, et al., Research Methods in Social Relations, rev. one-volume ed. (New York: Holt, Rinehart and Winston, 1959), pp. 336-370; and William J. Goode and Paul K. Hatt, Methods in Social Research (New York: McGraw-Hill Book Co., 1952), pp. 275-276.

item failed to discriminate between the low and high quartiles and was eliminated (see Appendix D). The traditional Chinese cultural orientation scale was used as independent variable.

The fifth part of the instrument of this study dealt with the respondents' demographic backgrounds: it asked questions about factors such as age, sex, place of birth, marital status, employment, income, religion, occupation, and so on. These demographic variables were used as independent and test variables in this study.

The interview schedule was translated from English to Chinese by two Chinese scholars. The Chinese translation by each scholar was then retranslated back into English by the other scholar to insure the reliability of the Chinese translation. One Chinese copy was then developed and served as the questionnaire by the interviewers while interviewing the Chinese speaking respondents. All of the answers made by the respondents were recorded on the English copy by another team member.

Pretest

Before the instrument was finalized, the research questionnaire underwent pretesting with fifteen Chinese workers or visitors in Chinatown to insure that the instrument was unambiguous and appropriate in style and content to the kind of information and responses needed to answer the major questions of this research. Few problems were encountered and no major revisions were necessary. Because it was a rather small pretest group it was not possible to conduct any kind of content or construct analysis of the items. Also, because most parts of the instruments were newly constructed for Chinese respondents in this study, the reliability and validity of the instrument are unknown.

Data Analysis

All of the data obtained in the interviews were coded and transferred to IBM computer cards for processing and analysis. The revised Statistical Package for the Social Sciences was used as the computer program for the data analysis. The computer processing was provided by the Computer Center at the University of Southern California.

The first stage of data analysis was to obtain frequency distributions for all of the variables in the study.

The second stage of data analysis was to construct two new variables (the acceptance scale and the traditional Chinese cultural orientation scale). The acceptance scale was considered to be one of the mental health judgment variables. The traditional Chinese cultural orientation scale was used as the major independent variable.

In the third stage of data analysis, nonparametric statistics were used to measure the probability of associations between the respondents' cultural orientation and mental health judgments. Categories of responses of each item were collapsed on an empirical basis to facilitate the data analysis. Appropriate statistical measurements, such as the chi-square test of significance and phi contingency coefficient, were adopted to analyze and explain the results. The conventional 0.05 level of statistical significance was used.

In the fourth stage of data analysis, the original significant relationships between participants' cultural orientation and their mental health judgments were examined with the introduction of selected personal characteristics as test variables. Each subsample of the test variable was compared with the original relationship to see whether or not the original relationships remained, diminished, or disappeared.

Considering that the survey was conducted by interview teams in the field, the responses were remarkable in their completeness. Therefore, there is no reference made to missing data in any of the tables presented. However, the number of missing data can be easily identified by subtracting the base number from the table of one hundred in the sample.

CHAPTER III

DESCRIPTION OF RESPONDENTS

This chapter describes the characteristics of those who participated in this study. Fourteen characteristics, following roughly into four major categories, are reported: (1) personal background, (2) occupational situation, (3) educational history, and (4) financial and housing condition. All of these descriptive items were used as independent variables in this study; some of them were also utilized as test factors in multivariate analysis.

Although households were selected by random procedures, individual respondents were not. Instead, only adults were interviewed and they were not selected randomly when there were multiple adults in a household. Thus, findings related to individuals cannot be considered representative of the community population. Those findings that relate to household units, however, are believed to be descriptive of the New Chinatown population.

Personal Characteristics

Seven personal characteristics--sex, age, place of birth, generation (if American born), years in the United States (if foreign born), marital status, and religion--are summarized in Table 1.

Sex. Among the one hundred respondents, 51 percent were male and 49 percent were female.

Age. The respondents' ages ranged from 18 to 77 years; the mean age was 40.5 years and the median age was 39 years. Thirty percent of the respondents were between 18 and 30 years

TABLE 1

PERSONAL CHARACTERISTICS OF RESPONDENTS

Personal Characteristics		Percent	Number
Sex			
Male		51.0	51
Female		49.0	49
	Total	100.0	100
Age			
18 to 30 years		30.0	30
31 to 44 years		34.0	34
45 to 77 years		36.0	36
	Total	100.0	100
Place of Birth			
Foreign-born		88.0	88
American-born		12.0	12
	Total	100.0	100
Generation (American-born)			
First generation		66.7	8
Second generation		33.3	4
	Total	100.0	12
Years in U.S. (foreign-born)			
1 or less to 5 years		27.3	24
6 to 10 years		35.2	31
11 to 20 years		18.2	16
21 to 54 years		19.3	17
	Total	100.0	88

TABLE 1--Continued

Personal Characteristics	Percent	Number
Marital Status		
Married	79.0	79
Single	13.0	13
Widowed	6.0	6
Separated or divorced	2.0	2
Total	100.0	100
Religion		
No religion	60.0	60
Protestants	15.0	15
Ancestor worship	13.0	13
Catholics	8.0	8
Buddhists	4.0	4
Total	100.0	100

of age, 34 percent were between 31 and 44 years of age, and 36 percent were between 45 and 77 years of age.

Place of birth. The majority of the respondents, 88 percent, were foreign-born Chinese. The rest were American-born Chinese.

Generation. Among the twelve American-born respondents eight were first generation Chinese-Americans and four were second generation Chinese-Americans.

Years in the United States. Among the 88 foreign-born respondents, the length of their stay in the United States varied from less than one year to 54 years; the mean length of stay was 11.75 years. Twenty-seven percent of the respondents had been in the United States less than 5 years, 35 percent between 6 and 10 years, 18 percent between 11 and 20 years, and 19 percent between 21 and 54 years.

Marital status. Seventy-nine percent of the respondents were married, 13 percent were single, 6 percent were widowed, 1 percent separated, and 1 percent divorced.

Religion. Of the respondents, 60 percent stated they did not have any religion, 15 percent were Protestants, 13 percent worshiped their ancestors, 8 percent were Catholics, and 4 percent were Buddhists. The large percentage of non-religious respondents may well reflect the actuality that Chinese people have never formed nor believed in the kind of super natural beings upon which Westerners have established their religions. With the exception of ancestor worship, which most Chinese do not consider a religion, all of the religions practiced by the Chinese are imported.

Occupational Situations

A modified form of the occupational scale developed by Hollingshead in his two-factor index of social position was used to determine and classify the occupationsl positions of the respondents in the study.[1] The differences among these

---

[1] August B. Hollingshead, "The Two Factor Index of Social Position," New Haven, Conn.: By the author, 1957. (Mimeographed.)

37

occupational categories are presumed to reflect the skill and power individuals possess as they perform the many maintenance functions in society. The occupations of the respondents were classified into ten different categories: major professional, lesser professional, small business owner, skilled manual employee, skilled mechanical employee, semi-skilled employee, clerical and sales worker, unskilled employee, housewife, and student.

Major professionals and lesser professionals together accounted for about 12 percent of the respondents; small business owners, 8 percent; skilled manual and mechanical employees jointly, about 10 percent. The largest occupational group was composed of semi-skilled employees; 31 percent of the respondents had such occupations. Twelve percent were clerical and sales workers, and about 5 percent were unskilled. The remaining 22 percent were housewives or students (Table 2).

Of the respondents, 70 percent were employed at the time of the survey. The rest were composed of housewives, students, and unemployed persons. Among the 79 respondents who were married, 68 percent had spouses who were employed.

Educational History

Educational history in this study included the total years of formal education received and place of education (Table 3).

The respondents' formal education ranged from less than one year to 22 years, the mean length of education was 10.6 years. Twenty-nine percent of the respondents had an education of six years or less, 24 percent had between 7 and 11 years, 26 percent had 12 to 15 years, and 21 percent had between 16 and 22 years of schooling.

When the place where respondents received their education was examined, it was learned that about 15 percent received all of their education in the United States. Fifty percent of the respondents received all of their education in foreign countries (any country that is out of the United States) and 34 percent of the respondents were educated both in the United States and foreign countries. Only 1 percent did not have any formal education.

TABLE 2

RESPONDENTS' OCCUPATIONS

Occupation	Percent	Number
Professional	4.0	4
Lesser professional	8.2	8
Small business owner	8.2	8
Skilled manual employee	4.1	4
Skilled mechanical employee	6.1	6
Semi-skilled employee	30.6	30
Clerical and sales worker	12.2	12
Unskilled employee	5.1	5
Housewife	13.3	13
Student	8.2	8
Total	100.0	98

TABLE 3

EDUCATIONAL HISTORY OF RESPONDENTS

Educational History	Percent	Number
Years of Education		
6 years or less	29.3	29
7 to 11 years	24.2	24
12 to 15 years	25.3	25
16 to 22 years	21.2	21
Total	100.0	99
Place of Education		
United States only	15.3	15
Foreign country only	50.0	50
Both U.S. and foreign country	33.7	33
No formal education	1.0	1
Total	100.0	99

Financial and Housing Conditions

Three variables were used to measure the respondents'
financial and housing conditions in this study. These characteristics are summarized and reported in Table 4.

The first variable was the respondents' major source
of income. The majority of the respondents, 84 percent, were
supported primarily by income received from employment; 7 percent depended on their children or relatives for support; 6
percent received benefits from the Social Security Administration; and 2 percent from retirement. Only 1 percent received
income support from the public welfare programs.

The second variable was the respondents' gross family
income for the year of 1974. The respondents' family income
ranged from less than $3,000 to over $25,000, with the mean
income of $11,073.68. About 5 percent earned below $3,000;
about 15 percent had family incomes between $3,000 and $6,000;
about 35 percent indicated a family income between $6,000 and
$10,000; about 25 percent were earning between $10,000 and
$15,000; about 8 percent had family incomes between $15,000 and
$20,000 and another 8 percent between $20,000 and $25,000. Only
3 percent reached a family income of $25,000 or over.

The third variable is home ownership by the respondents.
The majority of the respondents, 78 percent, rented their houses
or apartments. Twenty-two percent owned their houses.

In summary, the typical Chinese-American who participated
in this study was foreign born (88 percent), about 40 years of
age (the mean age of this sample was 40.5 years and the median
age was 39), male (51 percent male and 49 percent female), and
had lived in the United States for about 12 years (the mean
length of stay for foreign-born group was 11.75 years). Most
likely the respondent was married (79 percent), had no religion
(60 percent), had about 11 years of education in foreign
countries (50 percent), and worked as a semi-skilled employee
or clerical and sales worker (a combined 43 percent for these
two categories). Both the respondent and his spouse were employed (about 68 percent of the spouses worked) and together
they earned a family income of $11,074 in 1974. They were living
in rented apartments in New Chinatown (78 percent).

TABLE 4

FINANCIAL AND HOUSING CONDITIONS OF RESPONDENTS

Characteristics	Percent	Number
Major Source of Income		
Employment	84.0	84
Relatives	7.0	7
Social Security benefits	6.0	6
Retirement	2.0	2
Public welfare	1.0	1
Total	100.0	100
Family Income of 1974		
$ 3,000 or less	5.3	5
3,000 to $ 6,000	14.7	14
6,000 to 10,000	34.7	33
10,000 to 15,000	25.3	24
15,000 to 20,000	8.4	8
20,000 to 25,000	8.4	8
25,000 or over	3.2	3
Total	100.0	95
Housing Situation		
Rent	78.0	78
Own	22.0	22
Total	100.0	100

CHAPTER IV

CHINESE-AMERICANS' PERCEPTIONS OF AND
METHODS OF COPING WITH MENTAL ILLNESS

Various ethnic groups manifest different perceptions of and methods of coping with mental illness. In other words, the beliefs among members of an ethnic group as to what constitutes mental illness and what is appropriate in the way of treatment are formed and supported by generally held cultural attitudes.[1] Thus, how a given culture defines mental illness and what its beliefs are about methods of restoring mental health are important to mental health practitioners.

The first research question of this study thus asks the following:

1. How do Chinese-Americans perceive and cope with mental illness?

2. Are Chinese-Americans' perceptions of and methods of coping with mental illness different from those of other ethnic or social groups?

To deal with the first part of the research question, Chinese residents of Los Angeles New Chinatown were asked to respond to four case vignettes of common mental disorders-- these vignettes portrayed persons suffering from paranoid schizophrenia, simple schizophrenia, obsessive compulsive phobic neurosis, and childhood behavior disorder (see Appendix B). These cases were adopted from those developed by Shirley Star.

---

[1]Talcott Parsons, "Illness and Role of the Physician: A Sociological Perspectives," _American Journal of Orthopsychiatry_ 21 (1951): 452-460; and Sebastian DeGrazia, _Errors of Psychotherapy_ (New York: Doubleday & Co., 1952).

The only changes made were to give the persons described Chinese names. The sequence in which the case materials were presented to respondents was randomly determined. After listening to each case vignette, respondents were asked three questions about how they perceived these people, two questions about how they would cope with these people, and one question about previous personal experiences with such people. Some of these questions had standardized alternative answers and the others were open-ended questions.

To answer the second part of the first research question, Chinese-Americans' perceptions and methods of coping with mental illness will be compared with those of previous studies. Hopefully, this will offer some insights into the differences of perceptions and methods of coping with mental illness between Chinese-Americans and other ethnic and social groups.

Perceptions of Mental Illness

The respondents' perceptions of mental illness were examined in three ways. First, they were asked if they thought there was anything wrong with a person described in a vignette. If the responses were positive, then the respondents were asked to indicate if the problem was some kind of mental illness and how serious the mental illness was. Second, the respondents were asked to specify the cause of or the reason for the mental illness. The assumption was that their views of the cause of mental illness would reveal certain aspects of their perceptions of mental illness. Third, it was believed that having the respondents describe their previous experiences with four distinctly different types of mental illness would allow assessment of their overall understanding and awareness of mental illness.

The respondents' responses to this first approach to assessing their perceptions of mental illness are presented in Table 5.

When the respondents were asked if there was anything wrong with each particular case, 96 percent of them perceived the paranoid schizophrenic person as having something wrong, 74 percent of them perceived something to be wrong with the simple schizophrenic person, 40 percent of them perceived the obsessive phobic neurotic person as having something wrong, and 68 percent of them perceived the bahaviorally disordered child as having something wrong.

When the respondents were further asked to indicate if those people were mentally ill, 89 percent indicated that the

TABLE 5

RESPONDENTS' PERCEPTIONS OF MENTAL ILLNESS

Types of Mental Illness

Questions Asked	Paranoid Schizophrenia	Simple Schizophrenia	Obsessive Phobic Neuroses	Childhood Behavior Disorder
Anything wrong?	(N=100)	(N=100)	(N=100)	(N=100)
Yes	96%	74%	40%	68%
Mentally ill?	(N=100)	(N=100)	(N=100)	(N=100)
Yes	89%	50%	20%	19%
How serious is this mental illness?	(N=89)	(N=50)	(N=20)	(N=19)
Extremely serious	31.5%	12.0%	- -	10.5%
Moderately serious	42.7	28.0	10.0%	52.6
Mildly serious	23.6	48.0	45.0	15.8
Not serious at all	2.2	12.0	45.0	21.1

45

paranoid schizophrenic person was mentally ill and 50 percent of them stated that the simple schizophrenic person was mentally ill. Only 20 percent of them, however, thought that the obsessive phobic neurotic person was mentally ill and only 19 percent of them perceived the behaviorally disordered child as mentally ill.

When the respondents were asked about the severity of each particular mentally ill person, their responses were noticeably different from case to case. In the vignette describing a person with paranoid schizophrenia, 32 percent of the respondents considered the condition to be extremely serious, 43 percent moderately serious, 24 percent mildly serious, and 2 percent not serious at all. The respondents perceived the person with simple schizophrenia to be much less seriously ill. Only 12 percent of them regarded that person to be extremely serious. Twenty-eight percent saw the situation as moderately serious, 48 percent as mildly serious, and the rest, 12 percent, perceived the problem as not serious at all. When asked about the person with obsessive phobic neurosis no respondent considered his problem to be extremely serious. Only 10 percent of the participants saw the situation as moderately serious, 45 percent mildly serious, and another 45 percent not serious at all. As for the person with a childhood behavior disorder, 11 percent of the respondents thought his condition to be extremely serious, 53 percent moderately serious, 16 percent mildly serious, and 21 percent not serious at all.

As was mentioned in the introduction, behavior viewed as deviant in one cultural group may be seen as acceptable in another. In other words, how particular behavior is perceived or evaluated depends largely on the frame of reference the evaluators assume. Whether a particular behavior is seen as evidence of "mental illness," "crime," "wrong-doing," or so forth will be contingent on the criteria with which the examiner operates and how he applies them.

The respondents' responses to the four distinctly different persons described to them were assumed to reflect the criteria or framework that were used by Chinese-Americans in evaluating persons defined as mentally ill by American mental health professionals. In the following section, attempts are made to interpret the response patterns of Chinese-American respondents in this study. Hopefully, through this procedure will provide some understanding about how Chinese-Americans perceive mental illness.

The vast majority of the respondents (89 percent) perceived the person with paranoid schizophrenia. He was also more likely to be seen as seriously disturbed than were those with other types of mental illness. These findings suggest that Chinese-Americans tend to have low tolerance for those who show behavioral patterns of suspicion, mistrust, irrationality, and violence.

The respondents had more tolerance for a person with simple schizophrenia (only 50 percent saw him as mentally ill). In addition, this condition was less likely to be seen as serious. Thus, persons who are so withdrawn or shy that she or he is constantly daydreaming and afraid to participate in productive activities will be considered as mentally ill by only half of the Chinese-American population.

Relatively few respondents (20 percent) considered the person with an obsessive compulsive phobic neurosis to be mentally ill. They also perceived her mental condition to be mildly serious or not serious at all. In other words, Chinese-Americans did not think it was terribly bad or a sign of mental illness when a person was "extremely cautious" and displayed compulsive behaviors such as going back to see whether the stove was shut off or the door closed. On occasion, elevators do get stuck or are out of order; therefore, some of the respondents felt it was all right for people not to ride up and down in elevator sometimes. A good number of respondents stated that it is a good habit to be "cautious," particularly, if one is living in a "strange or foreign land."

Only a very few of the respondents (19 percent) perceived the twelve-year-old young boy with disordered behavior to be mentally ill. In addition, his mental condition was not considered to be a serious one. This suggests that Chinese-Americans tend to have considerable tolerance for children's mischievous or incorrigible behavior, and to interpret it as "bad" but not "sick."

The second approach to examining the respondents' perceptions of mental illness consisted of asking them to indicate the cause of the mental problem in each case. These responses believed to reveal additional aspects of their perceptions of mental illness. For example, would they consider mental illness to be the result of a physical illness, a psychological difficulty, a moral problem, or a drug or alcohol habit? The respondents' responses about the cause of mental illness in the four cases described to them are presented in Table 6.

The respondents' perceptions of the cause of mental illness differed markedly from case to case. For instance, when questioned about the person with paranoid schizophrenia, 35 percent of the respondents considered the cause to be mental and 33 percent perceived paranoid schizophrenia cause to be bad social and living experiences (victim of an assault, attack, tragedy, discrimination, and traumatic incident, etc.). The remaining respondents thought paranoid schizophrenia was related

TABLE 6

RESPONDENTS' PERCEPTIONS OF THE CAUSE OF MENTAL ILLNESS

Perceived Cause	Types of Mental Illness			
	Paranoid Schizophrenia	Simple Schizophrenia	Obsessive Phobic Neurosis	Childhood Behavior Disorder
Illness of mental basis	35%	9%	9%	1%
Personality defect or problem	6	38	21	7
Physical illness	..	2	..	..
Wrong peer group	..	..	..	20
Bad social and living experiences	33	16	16	4
Family conflicts	11	20	1	60
Moralistic problem	3	2	2	..
Drug or alcohol habit	4	..	..	..
Nothing wrong	2	8	50	4
Don't know	6	5	1	4
	100%	100%	100%	100%

to family conflicts, personality defects (shyness, passivity, aggressiveness, assertiveness, etc.), moralistic problems or drug or alcohol habits. In other words, the majority of Chinese-Americans tend to believe that the paranoid, acting out and violent person had an illness in his mind or that this behavior was the result of a bad social or living experience.

The respondents' perceptions of the cause of the simple schizophrenia were different, with 38 percent of them considering simple schizophrenia to be due to a personality defect or problem, 20 percent a family conflict, and 16 percent a problem in social and living experiences. Most of the respondents felt that the passive, immobile and daydreaming type of person described had some problem or defect in his personality or that this behavior was due to family conflicts or traumatic social or living experiences.

In the case of the obsessive phobic neurotic, about half of the respondents felt nothing wrong was with the person, about 21 percent of them thought the cause to be a defect or problem in his personality, and another 16 percent considered the cause to be related to bad social and living experiences. As a group, the respondents perceived the obsessive phobic neurotic person to be quite normal and it was a small minority who viewed him as having an intra-psychic problem.

In the case of the child with behavior disorder, the majority (60 percent) of the respondents considered the cause to be family conflicts. Another 20 percent considered the cause to be the influence of wrong peer group. Thus, in general, Chinese-Americans considered the family and the peer group to be responsible for the child's misbehavior.

The third approach to studying perceptions of mental illness asked the respondents to describe their personal experiences with any mentally ill Chinese-American. This was designed to reveal the extent to which the respondents had been exposed to mental illness. The results of the respondents' personal experiences with the mentally ill are presented in Table 7.

In the case of paranoid schizophrenia, 19 percent of the respondents stated that they had known or had experience with some Chinese-Americans who were like that. Twenty-one percent of the respondents had experience with Chinese-Americans who were like the case of simple schizophrenia. In the case of obsessive phobic neurosis, 43 percent of the respondents indicated that they had known some Chinese-Americans with the same problem. Thirty-seven percent of the respondents had personal experiences with some Chinese-Americans who showed symptoms of childhood behavior disorder. Given the less frequent occurrence of the

TABLE 7

RESPONDENTS' EXPERIENCES WITH MENTALLY ILL CHINESE-AMERICANS

Experience with Mental Illness	Types of Mental Illness			
	Paranoid Schizophrenia	Simple Schizophrenia	Obsessive Phobic Neurosis	Childhood Behavior Disorder
Yes	19%	21%	43%	37%
No	81	79	57	63
Total (N=100)	100%	100%	100%	100%

more serious mental disorders, these findings are not unexpec-
table and can be seen as partial evidence of the truthfulness
(validity) of obtained responses.

Methods of Coping with Mental Illness

This part of the study was designed to describe how
Chinese-Americans cope with mental illness. Respondents were
asked to indicate their coping methods by specifying the places
where they would go if someone in their family had the same
mental problems described in the case vignettes. It was believed that asking respondents to make recommendations of treatment or coping methods for their family members added some
emotional investment and personal involvement in the case conditions. In an open-ended question, the respondents were expected to give two recommendations for coping in each of the
case vignettes. This method allowed the respondents to give
free responses without limitations or restrictions. It was
assumed that the two recommendations for each case vignette
would indicate how the respondents would perceive and handle
mental problems in their own families.

The first recommendation of coping methods to each of
the four cases are described and presented in Table 8.

Eighty-nine percent of the respondents' considered the
paranoid schizophrenic to be mentally ill; yet, only 46 percent
recommended community mental health services and medical
facilities as the preferred method of treatment. Family relatives or friends were considered appropriate coping methods
also, and together they were recommended by about 21 percent of
the respondents. Social agencies, social clubs, churches, and
law enforcement agencies were suggested as appropriate resources
by about 18 percent of the respondents.

For the person with simple schizophrenia, a large number
(48 percent) of the respondents considered family relatives and
friends as the primary sources for treatment or help. This
recommendation suggests that Chinese-Americans are very likely
to try to handle withdrawn or immobilized persons within the
support of family members or friends. About 22 percent of the
respondents felt the person was ill enough to warrant psychiatric
or medical attentions. Only 13 percent of them would refer
simple schizophrenia to various social agencies or groups for
services or treatment.

For the person with an obsessive phobic neurosis, about
half of the respondents, 49 percent, stated that "no help was

TABLE 8

RESPONDENTS' FIRST COPING METHODS BY TYPES OF MENTAL ILLNESS

	Types of Mental Illness			
	Paranoid Schizophrenia	Simple Schizophrenia	Obsessive Phobic Neurosis	Childhood Behavior Disorder
Community mental health services	31%	11%	11%	2%
M.D. or hospital	15	11	3	3
DPSS or other social agencies	10	6	3	3
Social club	1	3	.	1
Church	3	4	1	3
Parents or relatives	16	44	23	66
Friends or neighbors	5	4	3	3
Law enforcement	5	.	.	4
School authority	.	.	.	10
No help needed	4	10	49	2
Did not know	10	7	7	3
Total (N=100)	100%	100%	100%	100%

needed," and 26 percent of them felt that relatives or friends would be able to assist him. Only 14 percent of the people would recommend psychiatric or medical services for the obsessive neurotic person. These patterns of recommendations clearly indicate that Chinese-Americans do not perceive obsessive compulsive neurosis to be a serious problem and would ignore it or handle it within the family or with friends.

For the boy with behavior disorder, 69 percent of the respondents preferred to solve the problem within the family or with the assistance of friends. About 10 percent of them would refer the child to school authority for discipline or assistance. Only 5 percent of the respondents considered him to need psychiatric or medical services.

In conclusion, the majority of the respondents rely very heavily on their parents and relatives, or even friends and neighbors, when dealing with mentally ill persons in the family. Mental health or medical services were preferred by a large proportion of respondents only in the case of paranoid schizophrenia. These results suggest that most Chinese-Americans would keep mental illness within the family system and not take advantage of the mental health services.

The second recommendation of coping methods was also examined to see what extent Chinese-Americans accept community mental health approaches to the treatment of mental illness. In other words, if the mental health service were not mentioned by the respondents as their first preference of treating the mentally ill family members, how many of them would consider it as their second choice?

In dealing with the person with paranoid schizophrenia, only 5 percent more of the respondents would consider mental health services as their second choice of treating this person (see Table 9). When their first and second recommendations are combined, 36 percent of the respondents would use mental health services as a coping method in treating a paranoid schizophrenic person.

In dealing with a person with simple schizophrenia, 8 percent more of the respondents would use mental health services as their second coping method. Combining the two recommendations together, there were only 19 percent of the respondents who would use mental health services as an approach to treating a person with simple schizophrenia.

In dealing with the obsessive phobic neurotic person, only 1 percent of the respondents would use mental health services as their second coping method in treating this kind

TABLE 9

RESPONDENTS' COPING PATTERNS BY TYPES OF MENTAL ILLNESS

Coping Patterns	Types of Mental Illness				
	Paranoid Schizophrenia	Simple Schizophrenia	Obsessive Phobic Neurosis	Childhood Behavior Disorder	
1st choice % recommending mental health services	31	11	11	2	
2nd choice % recommending mental health services	5	8	1	1	
Combined 1st and 2nd choice % recommending mental health services	36	19	12	3	

54

of mental illness. When the first and second recommendations were added together, only 12 percent of the respondents would use mental health services.

In dealing with the person with childhood behavior disorder only 1 percent more of the respondents would consider mental health services as their second coping method in treating anyone with this kind of mental problem. When the two recommendations were combined, the total percentage who had recommended mental health services for persons with childhood behavior disorder was only three.

Comparison with Other Studies

To answer the question of how Chinese-Americans compare with those from other ethnic or social groups, the results of this study will be compared with those of the others. As was discussed in Chapter II, only four out of the six mental cases in the Star instruments were used in this study. To make these vignettes realistic for the population under study, the persons described were given common Chinese names. In all other aspects, the case materials were unchanged.

Star's six case vignettes, in part or in whole, have been used many times, in different geographical areas and with different ethnic groups. In the following section, attempts were made to compare the results of this study with similar studies that have been conducted elsewhere with different populations (see Table 10).

Shirley Star conducted her original study of public attitudes toward mental illness with a national random sample of 3,500 adults in the early 1950s.[2] She found that 75 percent of the sample could identify the person with paranoid schizophrenia. The figure is slightly lower than the percentage of 89 found in this study. A similar trend is also indicated in the case of simple schizophrenia-- 34 percent of the sample of the Star study could identify the person as mentally ill in comparison with 50 percent of the respondents in this study. The percentages for the other two cases were not reported.

---

[2]Shirley A. Star, "The Public's Ideas about Mental Illness," paper presented at the Meeting of the National Association of Mental Health, Indianapolis, Indiana, November 5, 1955.

TABLE 10

PERCENTAGE OF RESPONDENTS IN THIS AND OTHER STUDIES WHO IDENTIFIED MENTAL ILLNESS
IN FOUR DIAGNOSTIC CATEGORIES

Population Studied	Types of Mental Illness			
	Paranoid Schizophrenia	Simple Schizophrenia	Compulsive Phobic Neurosis	Childhood Behavior Disorder
Chinese-Americans of Los Angeles Chinatown (Chen, 1975)	89	50	20	19
National sample of Americans (Star, 1950s)	75	34	..	..
Community leaders of New York City (Dohrenwend, 1960)	100	72	40	50
Residents of Baltimore City (Lemkau, 1960)	91	78	..	..
Residents of a Canadian town (Cumming, 1956)	69	36	..	..

However, there were other studies that seemed to show a rather different picture. In 1960, Dohrenwend, Bernard, and Kolb asked ninety-one community leaders in New York City to respond to Star's case vignettes.[3] In every diagnostic category, a higher percentage of respondents recognized the described behavior as mental illness than was the case in the study by Star or this study of Chinese-Americans.

Lemkau and Crocetti used only three of the Star case vignettes (simple schizophrenia, paranoid schizophrenia, and alcoholic) with a randomly selected sample of 1,736 in the city of Baltimore in 1960 and found that 91 percent of their sample could identify the paranoid schizophrenic as mentally ill.[4] This is similar to the findings of this study. But in the situation describing a person with simple schizophrenia, a much higher percentage of the Baltimore respondents, 78 percent, perceived the person to be mentally ill than was true for the Chinese-Americans (only 50 percent identified the simple schizophrenic as mentally ill).

Elaine Cumming and John Cumming who adopted Star's instruments, studied a randomly selected sample of 540 in a Canadian town and found that only 69 percent of their respondents were able to identify the paranoid schizophrenic and 36 percent the simple schizophrenic.[5] This study suggests that Chinese-Americans are more likely than Canadians to correctly identify paranoid schizophrenia as mental illness, but no more likely to correctly identify simple schizophrenia.

The findings of these studies were somewhat inconsistent. However, they did indicate some differences among people with different social, economic, and cultural backgrounds in their perceptions of mental illness. The comparisons between the results of this study and other studies of public attitudes toward mental illness revealed that Chinese-Americans are

---

[3] Bruce P. Dohrenwend, Viola W. Bernard, and Lawrence C. Kolb, "The Orientation of Leaders in an Urban Area Toward Problems of Mental Illness," The American Journal of Psychiatry 118 (February 1962): 683-691.

[4] Paul V. Lemkau and Guido M. Crocetti, "An Urban Population's Opinion and Knowledge about Mental Illness," The American Journal of Psychiatry 118 (February 1962): 692-700.

[5] Elaine Cumming and John Cumming, "Affective Symbolism, Social Norms, and Mental Illness," Journal of Psychiatry 19 (February 1956): 77-85.

relatively capable of identifying and perceiving mental illness,
particularly in the case of violent and acting out behavior.
However, they were less capable of identifying the milder form
of psychosis, neurosis, and behavior disorder of children.
Whether Chinese-Americans are similar to, or different from,
other ethnic minorities in what they define as mental illness
is unknown.

In the following section, attempts are made to compare
Chinese-Americans with others in terms of their recommendations
on how to cope with mental illness. Unfortunately, only one
of the previous studies asked respondents for their treatment
recommendations. The results of this comparison can be easily
seen in Table 11.

In the case of paranoid schizophrenia, only 36 percent
of the respondents in this study recommended mental health
services as a preferred method of treatment. This compares to
87 percent in Dohrenwend's study. For the person with simple
schizophrenia, only 19 percent recommended mental health services
in this study; while as in Dohrenwend's study it was 74 precent.
For the person with obsessive phobic neurosis, it was 12 percent
versus 46 percent. In the childhood behavior disorder case,
merely 3 percent of the respondents recommended mental health
services as a coping method as compared to 70 percent in
Dohrenwend's study. Thus, when compared with community leaders
in New York City, it is very clear that Chinese-Americans describe a pattern of underutilizing mental health services.

TABLE 11

PERCENTAGE OF RESPONDENTS IN TWO STUDIES WHO RECOMMENDED MENTAL HEALTH SERVICES
AS A METHOD FOR COPING WITH MENTAL ILLNESS

Population Studied	Types of Mental Illness				
	Paranoid Schizophrenia	Simple Schizophrenia	Obsessive Phobic Neurosis	Childhood Behavior Disorder	
Chinese-Americans of Los Angeles Chinatown (Chen, 1975)	36	19	12	3	
Community leaders of New York City (Dohrenwend, 1960)	87	74	46	70	

CHAPTER V

CHINESE-AMERICANS' ATTITUDES TOWARD, KNOWLEDGE ABOUT, AND PERCEPTIONS OF BARRIERS TO RECEIVING MENTAL HEALTH SERVICES

A review of the literature indicated that the mentally ill person is frequently perceived by the general public as deviant and, therefore, to be avoided. Studies have also shown that the "illness" or "medical" model has not been widely accepted by the public as a formula for understanding and treating deviant behavior. The public tends to place negative valuations on persons diagnosed as mentally ill. The public seems to be more tolerant of deviant behavior, however, when it is not described with mental illness labels. Because of the stigma attached to persons with symptoms of mental illness, individuals--especially those from social and cultural groups which label such symptoms as taboo--almost always try to keep these conditions hidden, and avoid seeking professional help.

The literature further revealed that the utilization of health services is highly related not only to the user's attitudes toward the services, but also to his knowledge about and perceptions of barriers to such services.

This chapter focuses on two research questions:

1. To what extent do Chinese-Americans accept Western concepts of mental illness and its treatment?

2. What are Chinese-Americans' knowledge about, attitudes toward, and perceptions of barriers to receiving mental health services?

Attitude Toward Western Concepts of
Mental Illness and Its Treatment

To answer the first research question of this chapter, ten items were constructed to test the respondents' attitudes toward Western concepts of mental illness and its treatment. Five of the items were related to the issue of the cause of mental illness and another five items were addressed to treatment methods. For the purpose of describing discrete as well as general understanding of the respondents' response patterns, the results are first presented separately (see Table 12) and then jointly in scale form.

When asked about the cause of mental illness, the majority of the respondents felt it was highly related to environmental conditions. For instances, 85 percent of them considered the cause of mental illness to be tension and trouble in the family and another 83 percent of them agreed that if the living environment was really bad anyone could become mentally ill.

When the cause was described in terms of individual moral weakness, few of the respondents indicated agreement. About 48 percent of the respondents considered the lack of will-power to be a cause of mental illness, while only 18 percent of them believed mental illness to be a form of punishment for sins.

When asked if mental illness was caused by genetic inheritance, 34 percent of the respondents agreed.

These findings reveal that Chinese people have a rather realistic viewpoint about the cause of mental illness. They most often agreed with the statement that bad environmental conditions can cause mental illness. The lack of will-power as a cause of mental illness earned the next highest amount of agreement; genetic inheritance came third, and punishment for sins was least often accepted as a cause of mental illness.

When referring to the treatment of mental illness, the majority of the respondents, 74 percent, had an optimistic expectation for the outcome. However, only 34 percent of the respondents agreed that a mentally ill person would recover faster if he were with his family. Furthermore, merely 23 percent of the respondents considered Chinese medicine as being effective in treating persons with mental illness. The majority of the respondents showed favorable attitudes toward Western methods of treating mental illness. For instance, 76 percent of the respondents agreed that counseling and psychotherapy are

TABLE 12

RESPONDENTS' RESPONSE PATTERNS TO WESTERN CONCEPTS
OF MENTAL ILLNESS AND TREATMENT

Items[a]	Response Patterns in Percentage[b]		
	Agree	Uncertain	Disagree
Cause of Mental Illness			
Mental illness usually comes from tension and troubles in the family	85	10	5
If the living environment is really bad; e.g., not enough money, no job, etc., anyone can become mentally ill	83	8	9
Mental illness usually arises from lack of will power	48	21	31
Mental illness usually is brought on as punishment for sins	18	22	60
Mental illness is usually inherited	34	27	39
Treatment Methods for Mental Illness			
Mental illness is usually curable	74	25	1
A person who has a mental illness is likely to recover faster if he is with his family	34	42	24
Chinese medicine is very effective in treating persons with mental illness	23	38	39

TABLE 12--Continued

Items[a]	Response Patterns in Percentage[b]		
	Agree	Uncertain	Disagree
Counseling and psychotherapy are very effective in treating persons with mental illness	76	20	4
Western medicine is very effective in treating persons with mental illness	64	24	12

[a]The order of the items has been rearranged for tabular presentation.

[b]To give a clear description of the response patterns to each item, the respondents' original responses were collapsed into three categories for tabular presentation. Those who responded strongly agree were grouped under "agree," while those who strongly disagreed were grouped under "disagree," and neutral responses were classified as "uncertain." The total number equals 100.

the most effective methods for treating Chinese patients, and another 64 percent of the respondents believed that Western medicine is a very effective means of treating mental illness.

The results of this portion of the study suggest that the Chinese, in general, indicate optimistic attitudes toward the outcome of treatment for mental illness. It is interesting to note that the Chinese do not show strong beliefs in either the family or Chinese medicine as appropriate or effective methods in treating mentally ill persons.[3] Instead, what was evident were favorable attitudes toward Western medicine as well as psychotherapeutic approaches.

Acceptance Scale of Western Concepts of Mental Illness and Its Treatment

As indicated in the methodology section, of the ten items discussed above, only seven items were retained to form the Acceptance Scale following the process of item analysis.[4] Because each item was itself a five-point rating scale, the total possible scores of the Acceptance Scale ranged from 7 to 35. The total scores of the Scale actually ranged from 13 to 29. In other words, no respondents had extremely positive or negative attitudes toward Western concepts of mental illness and treatment. The low quartile of the Scale actually ranged from 13 to 19, the high quartile ranged from 24 to 29, and the median was 21.313.

The median score of 21 was used to divide the respondents into two groups. About 53 percent of the respondents were considered to have more accepting attitudes toward Western

---

[3] The commonly held stereotype that the warmth and support of the Chinese family structure minimizes or decreases the degree of psychopathology is not supported by this study. Furthermore, the belief that Chinese-Americans perceive Chinese medicine to be effective in treating patients with difficult symptoms is not supported by this study.

[4] Three items were eliminated because they failed to reach a discriminative power of 0.50 between the scores of upper and lower quartiles. These three items are: (1) Western medicine is very effective in treating persons with mental illness, (2) if the living environment is really bad; e.g., not enough money, no job, etc., anyone can become mentally ill; and (3) mental illness is usually curable.

concepts of mental illness and treatment, and the other 47 percent to have less accepting attitudes.

The second research question concerned the attitudes, knowledge, and perceptions of barriers that Chinese-Americans have toward current services and resources in mental health. Five questions were constructed to test the respondents' attitudes toward mental health services, two questions were constructed to test their knowledge about current mental health services, and six questions related to barriers to receiving mental health services.

Attitudes Toward Mental Health Services

Among the five questions asked, the majority of the respondents expressed an overall positive attitude toward mental health services (see Table 13).

More than half of the respondents, 59 percent, agreed that a mental health clinic or agency can help Chinese who have mental or family problems. In this respect, it seems to reveal that a large number of Chinese do possess a rather positive attitude toward mental health services.

Almost all of the respondents, 92 percent, stated that they would encourage a friend or neighbor to go to a mental health clinic or agency to ask for help if he had a mental or family problem. A slightly smaller percentage of the respondents, 90 percent, indicated that they would encourage a relative or family member to go to a mental health clinic or agency for treatment if that person had a mental or family problem. It is interesting to note, however, that only about 73 percent of the respondents themselves would go to a mental health clinic or agency for therapy if they had a mental or family problem. This noticeable decline of percentage of respondents suggests that the less emotional involvement or attachment a respondent has toward a person, the more likely it is that he would recommend that person seek mental health services when the need arises.

A large majority of the respondents, 78 percent, thought that most Chinese-Americans would avoid going to a mental health clinic or agency for services even when they were in need of help. This finding supports the assumption that Chinese-Americans underutilize mental health services in Los Angeles County. The conflicting attitudes that the respondents have presented here between the first four questions and the last question can perhaps

TABLE 13

RESPONDENTS' ATTITUDES TOWARD MENTAL HEALTH SERVICES

Attitude Items	Percentage Agreeing (N = 100)
Mental health services can help Chinese with mental or family problems	59
Encourage friend or neighbor to use mental health services	92
Encourage relative or family member to use mental health services	90
Respondents would use mental health services	73
Chinese would avoid going to mental health services	78

be understood by looking at their knowledge about and perceptions of barriers to mental health services.

Knowledge About Mental Health Services

There are three major public or Short-Doyle contracted mental health hospitals and clinics available to Chinese residents in the Chinatown area.[5] These are the Resthaven Community Mental Health Center (hereafter referred to as Resthaven CMHC); the Los Angeles County South Center Mental Health Services (hereafter referred to as SCMHS); and the Los Angeles County-University of Southern California Medical Center, Psychiatric Outpatient Clinic and Inpatient Hospital (hereafter referred to as LAC-USC MC).

This section of the research first asked the respondents to identify mental health facilities known to them. If the respondents failed to identify any of the three mental health facilities serving their community, the interviewers then read to them the one(s) they had missed to see whether they could recognize it (them). It was hoped that through this double system of examination the respondents' true knowledge about the existing mental health services could be discovered. The results of the respondents' knowledge about these three mental health facilities are presented sequentially in Table 14.

TABLE 14

RESPONDENTS' KNOWLEDGE ABOUT MENTAL HEALTH FACILITIES
AROUND CHINATOWN AREA
(N = 100)

Name of Facility	Identifying	Recognizing	Identifying or Recognizing
Resthaven CMHC	44%	25%	69%
South Central MHS	1	3	4
LAC-USC Med. Ctr.	5	14	19

[5]According to the current mental health policy, known as the Short-Doyle Mental Health Laws in California, mental health services to the people should be provided by either the local governmental agencies or through contracted private sectors. For instance, Resthaven CMHC is the Short-Doyle contracted mental health facility.

When the respondents were asked to identify any mental health clinic or agency where Chinatown residents could go for treatment, 44 percent of them were able to name Resthaven CMHC, only 1 percent mentioned South Central MHS and 5 percent identified LAC-USC Medical Center. After the interviewers gave the name(s) of the facility(ies) they had missed, 25 percent more of them were able to recognize Resthaven CMHC, 3 percent SCMHS, and 14 percent LAC-USC MC. The total percentages of recognition and identification by the respondents are 69 percent for Resthaven CMHC, 4 percent for SCMHS, and 19 percent for LAC-USC MC. The high rates of recognition and identification for Resthaven CMHC by the respondents are probably due to the following reasons: (1) the location of that Center is in the heart of New Chinatown; and (2) the publicity that the center has received through mass gatherings and/or news media over the years regarding issues, such as community participation on the Board of Directors, different treatment programs for Asian patients, bilingual and bicultural staff, a new director who is sensitive to Asian community problems, and so on. The findings also suggest that the respondents lack knowledge about mental health facilities outside the New Chinatown area.

Perceptions of Barriers to Receiving Mental Health Services

There were six questions addressed to the respondents asking about their perceptions of barriers to receiving mental health services. The results are presented in Table 15.

Only 8 percent of the participants in this study had mental health insurance coverage at the time of study. In other words, unless they had an income large enough to purchase services, 92 percent of them would have to depend upon public or Short-Doyle mental health resources whenever problems arise.

Fifty percent of the respondents felt that the three mental health facilities above-mentioned were close enough for the Chinatown residents to get there for services without much difficulty. However, the other half of them did not think those facilities were accessible to the Chinese residents. This suggests that transportation would be seen as a problem by about half of the Chinese residents if they were to seek mental health services.

The majority of the respondents, 63 percent, did not know how Chinese patients were treated at the local mental health facilities. Only 15 percent of them stated that the services to Chinese patients were of good quality, 14 percent said fair, and 8 percent said poor. This again suggests that most of the Chinese residents lack familiarity with existing mental health facilities.

TABLE 15

RESPONDENTS' PERCEPTIONS OF BARRIERS TO RECEIVING
MENTAL HEALTH SERVICES

Barrier Items	Percentage Agreeing (N = 100)
Had mental health insurance coverage	8
Mental health facilities close to Chinatown residents	50
Treatment of Chinese patients in local mental health facilities	
Good	15
Fair	14
Poor	8
Don't know	63
Respondents had used mental health services	6
Knowledge of other Chinese using mental health services	28
Problems anticipated by Chinese or potential patients	
Communication (language)	87
Financial (money)	78
Moral (losing face)	76
Information (where to go)	92

Only 6 percent of the respondents had used existing mental health services in the past. This figure indicates that very few Chinese-Americans have had direct and personal experiences with the mental health system. However, 28 percent of the respondents claimed that they had personally known some Chinese who had used services at one of those three mental health facilities.

When the respondents were asked about the problems likely to be encountered by Chinese going to a mental health clinic or agency for treatment, a lack of information received the highest recognition (92 percent), communication or language problems were second (87 percent), financial problems were third (78 percent), and moral problems (shame or losing face) were fourth (76 percent). These findings support the results of some previous studies about the social and health needs of Chinese-Americans. For instance, Ivy Lee conducted a survey regarding the utilization of social services by Asians in Sacramento, California in 1973.[6] Frances Wu studied Mandarin-speaking aged Chinese in the Los Angeles area in 1974.[7] Both of these studies revealed that a lack of information and language barriers were considered to be the two most critical problems when Chinese seek social and health services. It is important to note that the majority of the sample of this study also considered financial and moral problems as the barriers faced by Chinese-Americans seeking mental health services.

---

[6] Ivy Lee, A Profile of Asians in Sacramento, U.S. Department of Health, Education, and Welfare Grant No. IROIMH 21086-01, September 30, 1973.

[7] Frances Yu-ching Wu, "Mandarin-speaking Aged Chinese in Los Angeles Area: Social Services and Needs" (D.S.W. dissertation, University of Southern California, 1974).

CHAPTER VI

CHINESE-AMERICANS' CULTURAL ORIENTATION

AND MENTAL HEALTH

This chapter addresses the following research questions:

1. Are variations in the cultural orientation of Chinese-Americans associated with differential definitions of and methods of coping with mental illness, and with their attitudes toward, knowledge about, and perceptions of barriers to receiving mental health services?

2. If so, are the relationships between cultural orientations and these mental health judgment variables affected by selected personal characteristics of the respondents?

Chinese cultural orientation was selected as a primary independent variable because cultural orientations influence, if not completely determine, individuals' beliefs, attitudes, knowledge, and behavior. In order to obtain a composite measure of the respondents' cultural orientation, a scale was constructed which consisted of fifteen items. (Refer to Chapter II for details of scale construction.) Because each item was a five-point subscale, the total possible scores of the scale ranged from 15 to 75. Actual scores ranged from a high of 57 to a low of 18. Respondents were dichotomized into more traditional and less traditional Chinese cultural orientation groups; of the 100 respondents included in the study, 53 were categorized as having more traditional cultural orientation, and 47 as having less traditional cultural orientation.

The cultural orientation scale was then crosstabulated with selected dependent variables in the study.[1] Statistically

---

[1] Some dependent variables were not used because there was limited variability of responses to them. In other words, these variables were virtually non-dichotomous in their frequency distribution.

significant relationships between the cultural orientation scale and those dependent variables were further studied and elaborated by the introduction of five of the demographic variables as test factors.[2] Five specific characteristics were measured to obtain a picture of the respondents' personal backgrounds. Two of these characteristics, sex and age, were the basis identifying characteristics of the respondents. Family income was assumed to be an indicator of respondents' economic class and living and social conditions; these, in turn were anticipated to have an effect on both their attitudes and cultural orientation. Years of education and the place where they received their education were assumed to contribute to the development of social values, ethics, beliefs, judgments, etc. All of these five variables were used as test variables to help understand and/or interpret the original relationships between cultural orientation and those variables related to mental health judgments.

The elaboration model that was conceptualized by Kendall and Lazarsfeld served as a guideline in this study.[3] As they indicated, the test variable can be either antecedent (prior in time) or intervening between the independent and dependent variables. Variables such as sex and age can be considered variables of antecedent character. The variables of years of education, place of education and family income, are considered as intervening.

Before the multivariate analysis could be pursued it was necessary to understand whether the independent variable, the dependent variable, and the test variable were significantly related to one another. In other words, the test variable would have to show a statistically significant relationship with both the cultural orientation variable and any

---

[2] These five demographic variables were the following: sex, age, family income, years of education, and place of education. Ten other demographic variables were not used because they were deemed inappropriate or lacked enough variability of response. These variables were the following: place of birth, years in the United States, spouse's employment status, generation status of American-born respondents, marital status, respondent's employment, respondent's occupation, source of income, housing situation, and respondent's religion.

[3] Patricia L. Kendall and Paul F. Lazarsfeld, "Problems of Survey Analysis," in Continuities in Social Research, ed. Robert K. Merton and Pual F. Lazarsfeld (Glencoe, Ill.: Free Press, 1950), pp. 148-158.

of the mental health judgment variables in order to assume
that they were empirically related to each other. Then, the
relationship between the original two variables (cultural
orientation and any of the mental health judgment variables)
could be recomputed controlling for the test variable. (All
of the test variables were dichotomized into two subsamples
in this study.) The partial tables on the subsamples were
than compared with the original relationship discovered in
the total sample.

Whenever the partial relationships (relationships
showed in the partial tables) were essentially the same as the
original relationship, the results were considered a "replica-
tion." In other words, the original relationship was considered a "genuine" one.

However, if the test variables were of an antecedent
nature and the partial relationships were weaker or nonexistent,
the test variable was considered to have "explained away" the
original relationship between cultural orientation variable and
any of the mental health judgment variables. If the test variable was of an intervening nature, then the same kind of finding
was considered as "interpretation."

A fourth condition possible in the elaboration process
is called "specification." In this situation one partial relationship looks very much like the original relationship but
the second partial relationship shrinks or disappears. The
elaboration study in this chapter was conducted, analyzed, and
interpreted along the guidelines mentioned above. As Babbie
stated, "The elaboration model is a logical device for assist-
ing the researcher in the understanding of his data. A firm
understanding of the elaboration model will facilitate a
sophisticated survey analysis."[4]

The Effect of Cultural Orientations on
Perceptions of and Methods of
Coping with Mental Illness

The cultural orientation scale was cross-tabulated
with three perception or coping method factors which were viewed
as outcome or dependent variables.[5] These three dependent

---

[4]Earl R. Babbie, Survey Research Methods (Belmont, Ca.:
Wadsworth Publishing Co., 1973), p. 294.

[5]Twenty-five dependent variables were not used because there
was limited variability of responses to them by the total
sample, i.e., these variables were virtually non-dichotomous
in their frequency distribution.

variables were the following:

1. Does Beverly Chien (described as having simple schizo-phrenia) have some kind of mental illness?

2. How serious is the mental illness?

3. Where would you go for help for this simple schizo-phrenic (first and second recommendations were com-bined)?

Only one dependent variable, the coping method for the simple schizophrenic person, was significantly related to the cultural orientation scale. In other words, the respondent's more or less traditional cultural orientations did affect or dif-ferentiate their recommended coping method or treatment ap-proach, and this association between these two variables was beyond what might have been expected by chance (see Table 16).

TABLE 16

RESPONDENTS' CHINESE CULTURAL ORIENTATIONS BY OVERALL
COPING METHODS FOR THE SIMPLE SCHIZOPHRENIC

| Recommended Coping Methods | Chinese Cultural Orientation | | | | | |
| | More Traditional | | Less Traditional | | Total | |
	No.	Percent	No.	Percent	No.	Percent
Mental health services	5	11.9	14	34.1	19	22.9
Non-mental health services	37	88.1	27	65.9	64	77.1
Total	42	100.0	41	100.0	83	100.0

$\chi^2 = 4.623$; df = 1; P = .031; Phi = 0.265.

As a group those respondents who had a more traditional Chinese cultural orientation were less likely than respondents with less traditional Chinese cultural orientation to use mental health services. Thus, only 12 percent of the respondents with

74

a more traditional Chinese cultural orientation recommended
mental health services as a coping method for a person with
simple schizophrenia. This contrasts with 34 percent of the
respondents with less Chinese cultural orientation who recommended use of mental health services. In the recommendations
for non-mental health services as the coping method for the
person with simple schizophrenia, the order reversed itself.[6]
About 88 percent of the respondents with a more traditional
Chinese cultural orientation, recommended non-mental health
services. These differences were significant at the 0.05 level.
The value of Phi was 0.265, however, which indicates a moderately weak association between Chinese cultural orientation and
recommendation for treatment of a person with simple schizophrenia.[7]

When five selected personal characteristics were cross-
tabulated with recommended coping methods for the simple schizophrenic none of these pairs of variables reached an acceptable
level of statistical significance. In other words, none of these
five personal variables was strong enough to significantly affect
the original relationship between respondents' cultural orientation and their coping methods for the simple schizophrenic. Thus,
it can be concluded that those with a less traditional cultural
orientation are more favorable to the use of mental health services as the coping method for a person with simple schizophrenia
than are those with a more traditional cultural orientation.

The Effect of Chinese Cultural Orientations
on Knowledge about and Perceptions of
Barriers to Receiving Mental
Health Services

The Chinese cultural orientation scale was cross-
tabulated with thirteen factors related to the respondents'

---

[6]Non-mental health services consist of medical doctors, clinics,
hospitals, DPSS; social agencies, clubs, churches, family
members, neighbors, law enforcement agency, school authority, etc.

[7]The other two dependent variables (whether or not the simple
schizophrenic person had some kind of mental illness, and the
severity of the problem of simple schizophrenic person) just
missed being significantly related to the cultural orientation
scale. The direction of the differences in these two tables
are similar to that discussed above; that is, respondents who
had a less traditional cultural orientation were more likely to
perceive the simple schizophrenic person as mentally ill and to
rate the illness as more severe.

knowledge about mental health services and perceptions of barriers to receiving such services.[8] These thirteen factors were considered to be the dependent variables and were listed as follows: whether participants recognized Resthaven CMHC and LAC-USC Medical Center; perceptions of the closeness of mental health facilities to residents of Chinatown; perceptions of how Chinese patients are treated; opinions as to whether mental health services can help Chinese; whether respondents had knowledge about Chinese using mental health services; opinions as to whether Chinese would avoid going to mental health services; whether respondents thought Chinese would experience any or all of the following problems: language, finances, shame; and finally, opinions about ideal methods for treating Chinese mental patients, in terms of either medical approach or staffing. When the Chinese cultural orientation scale was cross-tabulated with all of the thirteen dependent variables, five of the relationships were found to be statistically significant. The Chinese cultural orientation scale was thus related to recognition of Resthaven CMHC, recognition of LAC-USC Medical Center, perceptions of geographical distance between mental health facilities and Chinatown, opinions about how Chinese patients are treated by mental health professionals, and opinions about ideal staffing patterns. The significant relationships between the Chinese cultural orientation scale and these five dependent variables are presented and interpreted as follows:

1. Recognition of Resthaven Community Mental Health Center

As a group, respondents with a more traditional Chinese cultural orientation were less likely than those with a less traditional Chinese cultural orientation to recognize the presence of the Resthaven CMHC (Table 17).

---

[8]Eight dependent variables were not used because there was limited variability of responses to them by the total sample, i.e., these variables were virtually non-dichotomous in their frequency distribution. These variables were the following: having health insurance coverage; having mental health insurance coverage; identifying South Central Mental Health Services; encourage friends to go for services; identifying private mental health practitioners; respondents themselves would use mental health services; information barrier, and transportation barrier.

TABLE 17

RESPONDENTS' CHINESE CULTURAL ORIENTATIONS BY RECOGNITION
OF RESTHAVEN COMMUNITY MENTAL HEALTH CENTER

Recognition of Resthaven CMHC	Chinese Cultural Orientation					
	More Traditional		Less Traditional		Total	
	No.	Percent	No.	Percent	No.	Percent
Yes	30	56.6	39	83.0	69	69.0
No	23	43.4	8	17.0	31	31.0
Total	53	100.0	47	100.0	100	100.0

$\chi^2 = 6.915$; df = 1; P = 0.0085; Phi = 0.285.

About 57 percent of the respondents with a more traditional Chinese cultural orientation were aware of the presence
of Resthaven CMHC, compared to 83 percent of the respondents
with a less traditional Chinese cultural orientation. These
differences were significant at the 0.01 probability level. The
value of Phi was 0.285, however, indicating that the association
was moderately weak. The pattern seen in the table indicates
that respondents with a more traditional Chinese cultural
orientation are less knowledgeable about the existence of Resthaven CMHC: this may be due to their lack of interest or involvement in the community affairs as compared to those with a
less traditional cultural orientation. For many years Resthaven
CMHC has been the target of some Asian groups because of the
lack of community participation in its decision making as well
as its failure to meet the mental health needs of the Asian
communities.

When those five selected personal characteristics were
cross-classified with recognition of Resthaven CMHC, two of
these variables, age and years of education, were found to be
statistically related to the dependent variable. These variables were then introduced as test factors.

When the age was controlled, the original relationship between cultural orientation and recognition of Resthaven CMHC remained the same in the older age group (40 to 77 years) but disappeared in the younger group (18 to 39 years). Thus, in the older age group, respondents' cultural orientations remained significantly related to knowledge about the existence of Resthaven CMHC. However, this relationship was not evident in the younger age group.

When years of education was introduced as the test variable, the original association between cultural orientation and recognition of Resthaven CMHC dropped significantly in both of the subsamples (see Table 18). For example, the value of Phi correlation coefficient is 0.285 in the total sample; whereas the value of Phi dropped to 0.082 in the less educated group (with education 11 years or less) and the value of Phi went down to only 0.008 in the more educated group (with education 12 to 22 years). Furthermore, the differences in percentages between the total sample and the subsamples are also evident, particularly, in the group of high education respondents. Since years of education is a test variable of intervening nature, it can be concluded that it is the relationship between cultural orientation and years of education that affected the recognition of Resthaven CMHC. As a group, respondents with a less traditional cultural orientation and more years of education are more likely to recognize the existence of Resthaven CMHC.

2. Recognition of LAC-USC Medical Center

As previously mentioned, respondent's cultural orientation was significantly related to their knowledge about the existence of LAC-USC Medical Center (see Table 19). Only 4 percent of the respondents with a more traditional Chinese cultural orientation were able to recognize the existence of LAC-USC Medical Center as compared to 36 percent of the respondents with a less traditional Chinese cultural orientation. The relationship between these two variables was significant at the 0.001 level. The value of Phi was 0.412 which indicates a moderate association. These findings suggest that those with less traditional cultural orientation are more involved in the American society and thus are more familiar with the mental health system or services outside Chinatown.

When years of education was introduced as the test variable, the original relationship between cultural orientation and recognition of LAC-USC MC (Phi = 0.412) remained about the same in the high education group (Phi = 0.39), but dropped considerably in the low education group (Phi = 0.254).

TABLE 18

YEARS OF EDUCATION BY CULTURAL ORIENTATIONS
BY RECOGNITION OF RESTHAVEN CMHC

High Education Group

Chinese Cultural Orientation

Recognition of Resthaven CMHC	More Traditional	Less Traditional	Total
Yes	90.0% (10)	91.4% (32)	91.2% (42)
No	9.1% (1)	8.6% (3)	8.8% (4)
Total	100.0% (11)	100.0% (35)	100.0% (46)

$\chi^2 = 0.314$; df = 1; P = 0.575;
Phi = 0.008

Low Education Group

Chinese Cultural Orientation

Recognition of Resthaven CMHC	More Traditional	Less Traditional	Total
Yes	48.7% (19)	58.3% (7)	52.0% (26)
No	51.3% (20)	41.7% (5)	48.0% (25)
Total	100.0% (39)	100.0% (12)	100.0% (51)

$\chi^2 = 0.064$; df = 1; P = 0.8007;
Phi = 0.082

TABLE 19

RESPONDENTS' CULTURAL ORIENTATIONS BY RECOGNITION
OF LAC-USC MEDICAL CENTER

| Recognition of LAC-USC MC | Chinese Cultural Orientation | | | | | |
| | More Traditional | | Less Traditional | | Total | |
	No.	Percent	No.	Percent	No.	Percent
Yes	2	3.8	17	36.2	19	19.0
No	51	96.2	30	63.8	81	81.0
Total	53	100.0	47	100.0	100	100.0

χ^2 = 14.998; df = 1; P = 0.0001; Phi = 0.412

Thus, among respondents of the low education group, the lack of education seemed to be the primary influence on their knowledge about the existence of LAC-USC MC; while among respondents of the high education group, knowledge about the existence of LAC-USC MC varied depending on respondents' cultural orientation.

When the place of education was introduced as the test variable, the strength of the relationship between cultural orientation and recognition of LAC-USC MC turned out to be very similar for both the foreign educated group as well as those who received at least some of their education in the United States.

3. The Proximity of Mental Health
   Facilities to Chinatown Residents

The Chinese cultural orientation scale was found to be significantly related to the respondents' opinions about the geographic closeness of mental health facilities (Resthaven CMHC, SCMHS, and LAC-USC Medical Center) to Chinatown residents. When asked if these three mental health facilities were close enough for Chinatown residents to go for services, respondents with a less traditional Chinese cultural orientation tended to show more agreement than the respondents with a more traditional Chinese cultural orientation (see Table 20).

TABLE 20

RESPONDENTS' CULTURAL ORIENTATIONS BY OPINIONS ABOUT
FACILITIES CLOSE TO CHINESE RESIDENTS

Mental Health Facilities Close to Chinatown Residents	Chinese Cultural Orientation					
	More Traditional		Less Traditional		Total	
	No.	Percent	No.	Percent	No.	Percent
Agree	19	35.8	31	66.0	50	50.0
Disagree	34	64.2	16	34.0	50	50.0
Total	53	100.0	47	100.0	100	100.0

$\chi^2 = 7.868$; df = 1; P = 0.005; Phi = 0.30

Thus, 66 percent of the respondents with a less traditional Chinese cultural orientation, compared to 36 percent of
the respondents with a more traditional Chinese cultural orientation, thought those mental health facilities were close to
Chinatown residents. The relationship between these two variables was statistically significant at the 0.01 level with a
Phi value of 0.30 (moderate association). This relationship
suggests that as the commitment to a traditional Chinese
cultural orientation decreased, respondents were more likely to
think these mental health facilities were close to Chinese
residents in Chinatown.

Three of the five variables selected as potential test
variables were significantly related to this dependent variable.
They were age, years of education, and place of education.

When age was introduced as a test factor, the original
relationship between cultural orientation and knowledge about
mental health facilities close to Chinatown residents diminished
significantly in the younger age group (18 to 39 years) but
increased considerably in the older age group (40 to 77 years).
Therefore, in the older age group respondents with a less traditional Chinese cultural orientation were more likely to believe
that mental health facilities were close to Chinatown residents
than were respondents with a more traditional Chinese cultural
orientation. However, in the younger age group, cultural
orientation did not have a significant association with opinions
about the closeness of mental health facilities.

When years of education was introduced as the control
variable, the original association between cultural orientation and the knowledge about facilities as being close to
Chinatown residents dropped significantly in both the low education group (11 years or less) and the high educational group
(12 to 22 years) (see Table 21). For example, the difference
in percentages in the original table is about 28, whereas the
differences in the subsample tables dropped to about 21 in the
low education group and about zero in the high education group.
Furthermore, the value of Phi correlation coefficient in the
total sample is 0.30. The value of Phi dropped to 0.196 in the
less educated group and to 0.012 in the more educated group.
Since years of education can be assumed as a variable of intervening nature, it may be concluded that for those respondents
with more education, the closeness of mental health facilities
to Chinatown residents is probably a factual question. Because
they are better educated, they are more likely to know about
the existence of Resthaven CMHC and other mental health facilities. Those respondents who have less education were probably
less likely to know where those mental health facilities are
located. However, the question of whether or not mental health
facilities are close to Chinatown residents might be a matter
of opinion or speculation for those with less education.

TABLE 21

YEARS OF EDUCATION BY CULTURAL ORIENTATIONS BY MENTAL HEALTH
FACILITIES CLOSE TO CHINATOWN RESIDENTS

High Education Group

Chinese Cultural Orientation

Mental Health Facilities Close to Chinatown Residents	More Traditional	Less Traditional	Total
Yes	72.7% (8)	71.4% (25)	39.4% (33)
No	27.3% (3)	28.6% (10)	60.6% (13)
Total	100.0% (11)	100.0% (35)	100.0% (46)

$\chi^2 = 0.09024$; df = 1; Phi = 0.0123
P = 0.7639 (NS);

Low Education Group

Chinese Cultural Orientation

Mental Health Facilities Close to Chinatown Residents	More Traditional	Less Traditional	Total
Yes	28.2% (11)	50.0% (6)	33.3% (17)
No	71.8% (28)	50.0% (6)	66.7% (34)
Total	100.0% (39)	100.0% (12)	100.0% (51)

$\chi^2 = 1.10336$; df = 1; Phi = 0.19612
P = 0.2936 (NS);

83

When place of education was introduced as the test variable, the original relationship between cultural orientation and opinions about the proximity of mental health facilities remained about the same in the subsample of those who received education in foreign countries only. But the relationship dropped to almost zero in the subsample of those who had education both in foreign countries and in the United States. Thus, for the respondents who received only foreign education, the lack of educational experiences in the United States seemed to be the primary influence on perceptions of the closeness of mental health facilities. In contrast, cultural orientation tended to have more effect on the respondents who received education both in foreign countries and the United States. Thus, the original relationship between cultural orientation and opinions about mental health facilities as being close to Chinatown residents has been specified by introducing place of education as a test variable.

4. Treatment of Chinese Patients
   in Mental Health Facilities

As displayed in Table 22, the cultural orientation scale was significantly related to opinions about the quality of treatment received by Chinese patients in mental health facilities.

TABLE 22

RESPONDENTS' CULTURAL ORIENTATIONS BY OPINIONS ABOUT THE
TREATMENT OF CHINESE PATIENTS IN
MENTAL HEALTH FACILITIES

Treatment of Chinese Patients	Chinese Cultural Orientation					
	More Traditional		Less Traditional		Total	
	No.	Percent	No.	Percent	No.	Percent
Good or Fair	10	18.9	19	40.4	29	29.0
Poor or didn't know[a]	43	81.1	28	59.6	71	71.0
Total	53	100.0	47	100.0	100	100.0

[a]The rationale for combining the "didn't know" with the "poor" categories is the cultural practice that whenever something is bad or negative, Chinese people tend to express it politely by saying "don't know." Sixty-three percent of the respondents indicated they "didn't know" in the original frequency.

84

Nineteen percent of the respondents with a more traditional cultural orientation felt that the treatment of Chinese patients in mental health facilities was either "good or fair" compared to 40 percent of the respondents with a less traditional Chinese cultural orientation. Conversely, 81 percent of those with a more traditional Chinese cultural orientation and 59 percent of those with a less traditional Chinese cultural orientation perceived the treatment of Chinese patients as "poor" or said they "didn't know." The value of Phi was 0.237 which indicates a relatively weak association.

A suggested interpretation of this finding is that respondents with a less traditional cultural orientation are more knowledgeable about mental health services than those with a more cultural orientation. Therefore, they are more likely to know about the treatment of Chinese patients in mental health facilities. To the group with a more traditional cultural orientation, the question about treatment of Chinese patients might become a matter of opinion or their "didn't know" responses may be an honest declaration of ignorance.

When sex was introduced as a test factor, the original relationship between cultural orientation and judgment about the quality of treatment received by Chinese patients held in the male subgroup, but not for the female subgroup.

Place of education was also found to be significantly related to this judgment variable. When it was introduced as a control variable, the original relationship dropped considerably for those respondents who had only foreign educations but remained the same for those educated in both the United States and abroad. Thus, place of education has specified the original relationship between cultural orientation and judgment of the quality of treatment received by Chinese patients in mental health facilities.

5. Ideal Method for Treating
    Chinese Mental Patients--
    Staffing

The Chinese cultural orientation scale was found to be significantly related to the type of staffing recommended as ideal for treating Chinese patients (see Table 23).

As shown in Table 23, 60 percent of the respondents with less Chinese cultural orientation, but only 6 percent of the respondents with more Chinese cultural orientation, recommended Chinese professionals or qualified Westerners (those able to understand and accept Chinese people) as the ideal staff for treating Chinese mental patients. These differences were significant at the 0.0001 level with the Phi coefficient of

TABLE 23

RESPONDENTS' CULTURAL ORIENTATIONS BY IDEAL STAFFING
FOR TREATING CHINESE MENTAL PATIENTS

| Ideal Staffing Recommended | Chinese Cultural Orientation | | | | | |
| | More Traditional | | Less Traditional | | Total | |
	No.	Percent	No.	Percent	No.	Percent
Chinese professionals or qualified Westerners	2	5.6	24	60.0	26	34.2
No specific recommendations	34	94.4	16	40.0	50	65.8
Total	36	100.0	40	100.0	76	100.0

χ^2 = 22.594; df = 1; P = 0.0001; Phi = 0.573.

0.57301 (moderately high association). This pattern indicates that respondents with a more traditional Chinese cultural orientation show less familiarity with mental health treatment or less inclination to recommend Chinese professionals or qualified Westerners as the ideal staffing for treating Chinese mental patients than is the case with those with a less traditional Chinese cultural orientation.

When family income was introduced as a test variable, the original relationship between cultural orientation and the ideal staffing variable remained very much the same in both the high income group (those with an annual family income $10,000 and over) and the low income group (those with an annual family income of less than $10,000). Thus, the original relationship between cultural orientation and recommendations for the ideal staffing variable could be considered a valid one, unaffected by family income.

Similarly, when a second personal variable, years of education, was introduced as a test factor, the original relationship between the two variables remained very much the same in both the high and low education subgroups. Thus, the original relationship between cultural orientation and recommendations for ideal staffing for treating Chinese mental patients could be again considered as a genuine one.

When place of education was introduced as a test variable, the original relationship between cultural orientation and recommendations for ideal staffing held the same in both of the subsamples. Therefore, it can be concluded that the original relationship can be considered a genuine one.

Attitudes Toward Western Concepts of
Mental Illness and Its Treatment

The Chinese cultural orientation scale was cross-tabulated with the acceptance scale to see whether or not the respondents' Chinese cultural orientation was associated with their relative acceptance of Western concept of mental illness and its treatment. As indicated in Chapter V, the respondents were dichotomized into groups with more accepting and less accepting attitudes toward Western concepts of mental illness and its treatment. When the cultural orientation variable was cross-tabulated with this acceptance scale, the relationship was a statistically significant one (see Table 24).

As a group respondents with a more traditional Chinese cultural orientation showed more accepting attitudes toward Western concepts of mental illness and its treatment than did respondents with a less traditional Chinese cultural orientation.

TABLE 24

RESPONDENTS' CULTURAL ORIENTATIONS BY ATTITUDES TOWARD
WESTERN CONCEPTS OF MENTAL ILLNESS AND ITS TREATMENT

Accepting Attitudes Toward Western Concepts of Mental Illness and Its Treatment	Chinese Cultural Orientation					
	More Traditional		Less Traditional		Total	
	No.	Percent	No.	Percent	No.	Percent
More accepting	34	64.2	19	40.4	53	53.0
Less accepting	19	35.8	28	59.6	47	47.0
Total	53	100.0	47	100.0	100	100.0

$\chi^2 = 4.717$; df = 1; P = .0299; Phi = 0.237

About 64 percent of the respondents with a more traditional
orientation expressed more accepting attitudes toward Western
concepts of mental illness and its services, compared to 40
percent of the respondents with a less traditional Chinese
cultural orientation. These differences were statistically
significant at the 0.05 level of probability. The value of
Phi was 0.237 which indicates a moderately weak association
between cultural orientations and attitudes toward Western
concepts of mental illness and its treatment.

When five personal characteristics were cross-
tabulated with the acceptance scale of Western concepts of
mental illness and its treatment, only one variable, age, was
significantly related. When age was introduced as a test
variable, the original relationship between cultural orientation and acceptance scale remained the same in the younger age
group (18 to 39 years), but disappeared in the older age group
(40 to 77 years). The value of Phi correlation coefficient in
the younger age group was 0.436 which is higher than that of
the original sample group (Phi = 0.237), while the Phi correlation coefficient in the older age group dropped to almost zero
(0.059). Thus, the age variable specified the conditions under
which the original relationship holds. In the younger age
group, cultural orientation was the major influence in their
accepting attitude toward Western concepts of mental illness
and its treatment; while in the older age group, this was not
so.

Summary

This chapter examined the research question: Are
variations in commitment to a traditional Chinese cultural
orientation associated with differential perceptions of and
methods of coping with mental illness; with attitudes toward
and knowledge about mental health services; and perceptions
of barriers to receiving mental health services?

To answer this question, a 15-item cultural orientation scale was constructed and dichotomized and used as the
independent variable. Seven of the dependent variables emerged
to show significant relationships with the respondents' cultural
orientation. One of the dependent variables measured the
respondents' overall coping methods for a simple schizophrenic
person. Another one measured attitudes toward mental health
and mental health services. Four variables assessed the respondents' knowledge about mental health services. The last
variable assessed ideas about staffing for treating Chinese
mental patients.

The results of these findings are summarized as follows:

1. Those respondents with more traditional Chinese cultural orientations were less likely than respondents with less traditional cultural orientations to recommend mental health services.

2. Respondents with more traditional Chinese cultural orientations were less likely to know about the existence of Resthaven CMHC than were respondents with less traditional Chinese cultural orientations.

3. As commitment to a traditional Chinese cultural orientation decreased, respondents were more likely to know about the existence of LAC-USC Medical Center.

4. As traditional Chinese cultural orientation decreased, respondents were more likely to think those mental health facilities (Resthaven CMHC, LAC-USC Medical Center and SCHMHS) were close to Chinese residents in Chinatown.

5. The respondents with more traditional Chinese cultural orientations tended to show less favorable attitudes toward the treatment of Chinese patients in mental health facilities than did those with less traditional Chinese cultural orientations.

6. Respondents with a more traditional Chinese cultural orientation were less likely to recommend Chinese professionals and qualified Westerners as the ideal staff for treating Chinese mental patients than were those with a less traditional Chinese cultural orientation.

7. As a group, those respondents with a more traditional Chinese cultural orientation showed more positive attitudes toward Western concepts of mental illness and mental health services than respondents with a less traditional Chinese cultural orientation.

In summary, these findings suggest that cultural orientation plays an important role in determining respondents' perceptions of and methods of coping with mental illness as well as their attitudes toward, knowledge about, and perceptions of barriers to receiving mental health services. Their views of mental health, to some extent, are reflections of their differences in Chinese cultural orientation.

This chapter further examined the relationships between respondents' Chinese cultural orientation and seven of their mental health judgment variables by introducing five selected personal characteristics as the test variables. Two of these personal characteristics consisted of basic identifying information about the respondents, and three were assumed to measure the respondents' economic and educational backgrounds.

Thirteen out of a possible thirty-five relationships between these pairs of variables reached levels of statistical significance. No single variable of a personal characteristic was strong enough to significantly affect all seven mental judgment variables, nor was any judgment variable sensitive enough to be affected by all of the five personal characteristics. Two of the personal characteristics, years of education and place of education, showed most influence on respondents' mental health judgments. The next most influential characteristic was the variable of age. The least influential characteristic was family income of the respondent.

These five selected personal characteristics were introduced as test variables to determine if they influenced the original relationships between cultural orientation and the seven mental health judgment variables. This elaboration process provided clearer indications about how the respondents' personal characteristics influenced their mental health judgments (see Table 25).

Descriptive interpretations of the results in Table 25 are summarized and presented as follows:

Sex. In the male subsample, cultural orientation was the primary influence on respondents' judgment of the treatment for Chinese patients. This relationship did not hold among the female subsample.

Age. In the older age group, cultural orientation was related to knowledge about the existence of Resthaven CMHC, but this was not so for the younger age group.

In the older age group, perceptions of the proximity of mental health facilities to Chinatown residents were related to cultural orientations. This relationship did not hold for younger respondents.

In the younger age group, cultural orientation was the major influence on attitudes toward Western concepts of mental illness and its treatment. In the older age group, cultural orientation was unrelated to attitudes toward Western concepts of mental illness and its treatment.

Years of education. Respondents with more years of education were likely to have a less traditional Chinese cultural orientation but more knowledge about the existence of

TABLE 25

INFLUENCE OF SELECTED TEST FACTORS ON THE RELATIONSHIPS BETWEEN
CULTURAL ORIENTATIONS AND MENTAL HEALTH JUDGMENTS

Dependent Variables	Test Factors				
	Sex	Age	Family Income	Years of Education	Place of Education
Coping methods for simple schizophrenic	. . .	. . .	. . .	. . .	. . .
Recognition of Resthaven CMHC	. . .	Specification	. . .	Interpretation	. . .
Recognition of LAC-USC MC	. . .	. . .	. . .	Specification	Replication
Facilities close to Chinese residents	. . .	Specification	. . .	Interpretation	Specification
Treatment of Chinese patients	Specification	. . .	. . .	. . .	Specification
Ideal treatment staff for Chinese	. . .	. . .	Replication	Replication	Replication
Acceptance scale for mental illness	. . .	Specification	. . .	. . .	. . .

Resthaven CMHC when compared to respondents with less education. Among respondents with high education, cultural orientation appeared to have more effect on their knowledge about the existence of LAC-USC MC. This was not so for those with less education. In considering the proximity of mental health facilities to Chinatown residents, respondents with more education had less traditional cultural orientations and were more likely to consider those facilities as being close to Chinatown residents. The opposite was true for those with less education. Amount of education did not significantly affect respondents' recommendations about ideal treatment staff.

   <u>Place of education</u>. Place of education had no significant effect on respondents' ability to recognize the existence of Resthaven CMHC and LAC-USC Medical Center. However, the lack of educational experiences in the United States seemed to have a major effect on respondents' judgments about whether mental health facilities were close enough to Chinatown residents. When asked how Chinese patients were treated in mental health facilities, respondents with education in both the United States and foreign countries showed a less traditional Chinese cultural orientation and more positive opinions about the treatment of Chinese patients in mental health facilities than those respondents with education only in foreign countries. Place of receiving education did not seem to show any significant effect on respondents' recommendations on the ideal treatment staff for Chinese mental patients; cultural orientation remained more influential than place of education on recommendations for ideal treatment staff.

CHAPTER VII

CONCLUSIONS AND IMPLICATIONS

Introduction

The concept of mental illness and the treatment of mental illness, both in theory and in practice, vary greatly from culture to culture and society to society. Descriptions among members of a particular cultural or ethnic group about what constitutes mental illness and its treatment are formed and supported by generally held cultural attitudes.

In American society, the ways of defining and approaching mental illness/health have changed across the years. It was not until the early twentieth century that mental health practitioners adopted Freud's view of intrapsychic conflicts as the basis of mental illness and accepted his psychodynamic model for treatment. Although the current theory and practice of mental health services focus on community mental health, intrapsychic conflicts and psychodynamic ideas remain influential.

Many scholars and practitioners have indicated that mental health services focus upon the white middle class. Whether or not the current existing mental health services and programs can be accepted by members of other ethnic groups and sanctioned by them as an effective way of treating their mental health problems is an open question. This question has been debated not only by mental health practitioners but also by interested individuals and groups as well. Among professions, social work has been the one most interested and concerned about how social and cultural factors affect individuals' behavior and well-being. Social workers have also been involved extensively with the treatment of mentally ill and the development of programs to serve the mentally ill.

A review of the limited empirical, theoretical, and impressionistic literature on mental health services to minority groups revealed that various ethnic groups manifest different perceptions of and attitudes toward mental illness and suggested that prevalent mental health services may not be relevant to them culturally.

To conduct an empirical study on the issue of whether current mental health services are culturally relevant to all minority groups in the United States would be virtually impossible; appropriate research instruments do not exist and the expenses of time and money would be prohibitive. This study concerned a single, rather small ethnic group--Chinese-Americans-- and focused on two interrelated questions. First, what are Chinese-Americans' views of mental health--including their definitions of and methods of coping with mental illness, and attitudes toward, knowledge about, and perceptions of barriers to receiving community mental health services? Second, to what extent do Chinese-Americans' cultural orientations affect their mental health judgments? Both of these questions are of an exploratory nature and require empirical data to answer them. In order to fully answer the two major questions, data in this study were analyzed to respond to the following four specific questions:

1. How do Chinese-Americans define and cope with mental illness? Are their definitions of and methods of coping with mental illness different from other ethnic or social groups?

2. To what extent do Chinese-Americans accept Western concepts of mental illness and its treatment?

3. What are Chinese-Americans' attitudes toward and knowledge about existing mental health services, and what are their perceptions of barriers to receiving mental health services?

4. Are variations in the Chinese cultural orientations related to Chinese-Americans' mental health judgments? If so, are the relationships between respondents' cultural orientations and their mental health judgments affected by selected personal characteristics?

To answer these questions, one hundred households were randomly selected and adult residents were interviewed in New Chinatown of Los Angeles during the Summer of 1975. All of the respondents were asked to listen to four case descriptions. They were then expected to answer seven questions about each vignette and give their definitions of and methods of coping with such mental illness. Other questions were designed to deal with the research questions about Chinese-Americans' knowledge about, and perceptions of barriers to receiving mental

health services. Further, a Chinese cultural orientation scale
was constructed to differentiate respondents' cultural orientations toward either the traditional Chinese culture or the
dominant American culture. The last part of the questionnaire
was designed to provide information about respondents' personal
characteristics. Then, the traditional Chinese cultural orientation scale and personal characteristic variables were cross-
tabulated with those dependent variables to examine the relationships. Detailed description of the research methodology
and full summaries of the findings have been presented in earlier
chapters. In this chapter, summaries of the major findings will
be presented and followed by a discussion of implications for
mental health practice and policy as well as future research.

Although this study was done with a random sample, the
findings of this study must be restricted to the adult residents
of New Chinatown in Los Angeles. Generalizing the findings of
this study to other ethnic groups or Chinese in other Chinatowns
or communities must be done with caution.

How Do Chinese-Americans Define and Cope with Mental Illness? Are Their Definitions of and Methods of Coping with Mental Illness Different from Other Social Groups?

Summary

Chinese-Americans' definitions of mental illness were
assessed by asking respondents to identify if the persons described in four case vignettes were mentally ill. Eighty-nine
percent of them considered the paranoid schizophrenic person
mentally ill, 50 percent of them felt the simple schizophrenic
person was mentally ill, 20 percent of them thought the compulsive phobic neurotic was mentally ill, and 19 percent of
them perceived the behaviorally disordered child as mentally
ill. When compared with other ethnic or social groups in other
studies, Chinese-Americans are relatively capable of identifying the violent and psychotic person as being mentally ill.
However, they seemed to have more "tolerance" for passive, re-
gressive, neurotic, or childish types of behaviors. They did
not perceive these symptoms as severe enough to be defined as
mental illness. In other words, the Chinese subculture seems
to socially accept or protect a person with less extreme
symptoms, thus treating some types of mental illness within
the confines of the family and preventing some of the mentally
ill Chinese-Americans from becoming mental statistics.

When respondents' methods of coping with mental illness were examined by types of mental illness, community mental health services were not regarded as the primary or major treatment approach in any of the situations. Only 36 percent of the respondents recommended mental health services for the paranoid schizophrenic person, 19 percent for the simple schizophrenic person, 12 percent for the compulsive phobic neurotic person, and only 3 percent for the child with a behavioral disorder. Parents or family relatives were highly regarded as the major resource for handling mental problems in all of the four situations. It is obvious that the results of this study have confirmed the phenomenon of underutilization of mental health services by Chinese-Americans.

Implication

These findings indicate that Chinese-Americans perceive and define mental illness rather differently from some other cultural groups and have more "tolerance" for non-violent or less extreme types of mental illness. A possible solution in terms of policy or practice changes is to put special emphasis on community education. Hopefully, through this educational process Chinese-Americans will be able to perceive or define a variety of types of mental illness and seek treatment in the early stages before conditions become too severe and beyond treatment or restoration.

Two other implications related to mental health practice can be drawn from these findings. The first suggestion is in regard to the terms "mental illness" and "psychiatric" that are commonly used by mental health professionals. Evidently, Chinese-Americans consider only psychotic, violent, and acting out symptoms as indications of mental illness and perceive neurotic or behavioral disordered persons as being "bad" but not "mentally ill." In order to minimize the stigma, anxiety, and misunderstanding associated with a service program identified as "mental health" or "psychiatric," it may be advisable to use some neutral or culturally relevant names such as "family service center," "service center," and "children's services."

A second suggestion for practice is related to the improvement of the diagnostic capabilities of mental health professionals. In other words, mental health professionals, particularly those who are dealing with Chinese patients, should be more familiar with Chinese culture, values, and life styles, so that they can avoid making distorted diagnoses and offering unacceptable or inappropriate treatment to Chinese-Americans.

Chinese-Americans still depend very much on their immediate family system as the major resources for coping with their mental problems. They will not use outside mental health resources, unless it is necessary. This explains in part the underutilization of community mental health services by Chinese-Americans. One recommendation for a possible change of treatment approach with Chinese-American patients is to work more closely or directly with and through their family system. It is evident that the Chinese family is a cohesive unit. Its resources might well prove helpful in treating mental patients. A recommendation for future policy is the establishment of mental health units or programs within the existing Chinese neighborhood schools and social service agencies to provide services such as case finding, early prevention, and immediate intervention.

To What Extent Do Chinese-Americans' Accept Western Concepts of Mental Illness and Its Treatment?

To answer this research question, ten items were constructed. Five were related to the cause of mental illness and another five items were addressed to treatment methods. The findings revealed that Chinese-Americans have rather realistic notions about the cause of mental illness. They most often agreed with the statement that bad environmental conditions can cause mental illness. Lack of willpower, genetic inheritance, and punishment for sins were less often accepted as causes of mental illness. When referring to methods of treating mental illness, the majority of the respondents showed favorable attitudes toward Western methods of treating mental illness. For instance, 76 percent of the respondents agreed that counseling and psychotherapy are the most effective methods for treating mentally ill Chinese, and another 64 percent of them believed that Western medicine is a very effective means of treating mental illness. For the purpose of obtaining a general understanding of the respondents' acceptance of Western concepts of mental illness and its treatment, a seven-item Likert-type scale was constructed to answer the question. Because each item was a five-point scale, the total possible scores of the scale ranged from 7 to 35; the actual range was from 13 to 29. The median score of 21 was used to divide the respondents into two groups. About 53 percent of the respondents were considered to have more accepting attitudes toward Western concepts of mental illness and its treatment, and the other 47 percent to have less accepting attitudes.

Duplications

Despite the general assumptions or belief that mental health is a white middle-class activity, the majority of the respondents were found to have positive attitudes toward Western concepts of mental illness and its treatment. Although Chinese-Americans generally agree with Western approaches to the treatment of mental illness the acceptability and efficacy of specific approaches or treatment models need to be explored and studied further. In other words, an examination of the actual treatment of Chinese-Americans by these methods is necessary to determine whether or not the respondents' faith in Western approaches is warranted.

What Are Chinese-Americans' Attitudes Toward, Knowledge About, and Perceptions of Barriers to Receiving Mental Health Services?

Summary

The results of the six questions about the respondents' attitudes toward mental health services gave a clear indication that the majority of Chinese-Americans felt mental health services could help them with their mental or family problems and that they would encourage their neighbors, family members, and even themselves to use mental health services. However, only 6 percent of the respondents had used mental health services and a large majority of the respondents felt that most Chinese-Americans would avoid going to a mental health clinic for services when the need was indicated. Those findings suggest that most Chinese-Americans would not utilize mental health services even though they had expressed favorable attitudes toward the services.

Furthermore, 92 percent of the respondents did not have insurance coverage for mental health services. The majority of Chinese-Americans have to depend on public or Short-Doyle contracted mental health resources. A major problem is that the respondents' knowledge about the existence of available mental health resources as well as their perceptions of the quality of mental health services to Chinese-Americans were poor or negative.

Lack of information about available services was cited as the most critical barrier or problem that respondents considered when seeking mental health services. Next most important were language or communication problems and financial or money problems. It is important to note that the respondents in this study also considered shame or loss of face to be the crucial problem faced by Chinese seeking mental health services.

Implications

The findings of the respondents' attitudes toward mental health services seemed somewhat inconsistent. On the one hand,

Chinese-Americans expressed favorable attitude towards mental
health services and also believed such services would be
helpful to them. On the other hand, they believed that Chinese-
Americans would avoid using mental health services whenever
problems arose. These findings imply that believing is one
thing and practicing is another thing. Additional research is
required to examine the actual patterns of utilization of
mental health services by Chinese-Americans.

The majority of the respondents were not familiar with
existing mental health resources. This finding suggests that
lack of knowledge about mental health services by Chinese-
Americans may account in part for their underutilization of
mental health services. It is evident that the majority of
Chinese-Americans think they will encounter multiple problems
if they seek mental health services. Thus, underutilization of
mental health services by Chinese-Americans may be, at least in
part, due to the lack of information about resources and the lack
of bilingual capacity on the part of mental health professionals.
A suggested solution is the development of a highly visible community mental health service center that has an aggressive outreach program and a bilingual and bicultural staff. Hopefully,
a treatment setting of this kind will provide a milieu with more
cultural relevance for Chinese-American patients. It might re-
duce or eliminate some of the barriers that prevent those in need
from receiving community mental health services. Furthermore,
bilingual non-professional staff from the Chinese community might
be used as "bridge persons" and "expediters"; such community
workers might well reach out to those in difficulty, make home
visits, and follow up and follow through on treatment plans.

Another recommendation concerns the location of mental
health centers. Some of the respondents indicated that the
location of a mental health center should not be in Chinatown,
but rather somewhere near Chinatown. The rationale behind this
suggestion is that many who need mental health services do not
want to be seen or identified as "patients" by other Chinese
residents.

Another recommendation is to involve community people
in decision and policy-making processes. As was mentioned in the
assumption statement, the perceptions, attitudes, and identified
needs of community residents or potential consumers are valid
and important in program development and policy formulation. As
a matter of fact, the whole concept of community mental health
services was based on the assumption that a locally planned,
developed, and administered mental health service might best
meet community needs as well as have a better chance for local
support. Not only community or civic leaders, but also potential
or actual consumers, should be involved in on-going program
planning, administration, and decision-making. Their crit-
icisms and/or supports are necessary inputs if the real mental
health needs of the community are to be identified and met.

A fifth suggestion is the development of an information and support system utilizing the existing Chinese family
and tong associations. History and literature have indicated
that the Chinese family associations have traditionally provided social, economic, and spiritual assistance and supports
to its members. These family associations can play an important role in maintaining the mental well-being of its members,
both directly and indirectly. Some of the barriers perceived
by the respondents in this study could be easily resolved by
developing a mental health information and support system based
on the Chinese family structure strengthened with Western mental
health methods, techniques, and knowledge.

Are Variations in the Chinese Cultural Orientations Related to Chinese-Americans' Mental Health Judgments?

Summary

A 15-item Chinese cultural orientation scale was cross-
tabulated with all of the respondents' mental health judgment
variables in five specific areas: (1) perceptions of mental
illness, (2) methods of coping with mental illness, (3) attitudes
toward mental health services, (4) knowledge about mental health
services, and (5) perceptions of barriers to receiving mental
health services.

None of the perception-of-mental-illness variables were
significantly related to the Chinese cultural orientation variable. In other words, Chinese cultural orientation did not seem
to be statistically related to what Chinese-Americans define as
mental illness.

Chinese cultural orientation was significantly related
only to the methods recommended for coping with the simple schizophrenic. As a group, respondents with a more traditional Chinese
cultural orientation were less likely than the respondents with
a less traditional Chinese cultural orientation to recommend the
use of mental health services for the simple schizophrenic patient.

Variations in the respondents' Chinese cultural orientation were significantly related to acceptance of Western concepts of mental illness and its treatment. Respondents with a
more traditional Chinese cultural orientation expressed more
accepting attitudes toward Western concepts of mental illness
and treatment than did those with less traditional cultural orientations.

Cultural orientation was significantly related to five other variables. Two of these variables assessed respondents' knowledge about the presence of Resthaven CMHC and LAC-USC Medical Center. The other three measured respondents' knowledge about the geographical locations of the mental health facilities, opinions about the kind of treatment received by Chinese mental patients in those facilities, and opinions about ideal treatment staff for Chinese mental patients.

In combination, these five sets of associations suggest that as respondents' commitment to traditional Chinese culture decreased, they were more likely to know about the presence of existing mental health facilities, to show more favorable attitudes toward the treatment of Chinese patients in those facilities, and to express more familiarity with or inclination toward recommending Chinese professionals or qualified Westerners as the ideal staff for treating Chinese mental patients.

Implications

Several interpretations and implications are suggested by these findings. The first is that respondents with a less traditional Chinese cultural orientation are possibly more assimilated into the American society. Thus, they are more familiar with the resources and more inclined toward using mental health services. Having this knowledge and positive attitudes, they would tend to utilize mental health services more frequently. On the other hand, respondents with a more traditional Chinese cultural orientation tend to have limited knowledge about existing mental health services. This, in turn, may result in their underutilizing mental health services.

Commitment to traditional Chinese cultural orientations was not related to the respondents' definitions of mental illness nor was it related to their perceptions of barriers to receiving services. This finding suggests that, regardless of cultural orientation, Chinese-Americans share similar perceptions of what constitutes mental illness and they all perceive the same barriers to receiving mental health services.

Those respondents with a more traditional Chinese cultural orientation were more likely to have positive attitudes toward Western concepts of mental illness and its treatment than those with less traditional cultural orientations. This finding coincides with an earlier finding that despite the general belief that mental health is a white middle-class activity, Chinese-Americans accept mental health services as being the appropriate treatment for mental illness.

Considering all these findings, a conclusive statement about Chinese-Americans' mental health judgment is that they share similar perceptions and attitudes toward mental illness, but lack of information, and language and financial barriers have limited their utilization of mental health services. If these problems are to be solved, future programs must place special emphasis on bilingual outreach programs for those who do not speak much English, do not know about existing resources, are less assimilated into the American culture, and lack the financial resources to purchase services.

Are Relationships Between Chinese Cultural Orientations and Mental Health Judgments Affected by the Selected Personal Characteristics?

Summary

Five selected personal characteristics were introduced as test variables to explore the conditions under which the original relationships between Chinese cultural orientation and seven mental health judgment variables either held constant, diminished, or disappeared. These test variables were sex, age, family income, years of education, and place of education. Thirteen out of the possible thirty-five relationships proved to be statistically significant. No single test variable was strong enough to significantly affect all seven dependent variables, nor was any judgment variable sensitive enough to be affected by all five personal characteristics. Four out of the thirteen significant relationships were replications of the original relationships. There were seven specifications and two interpretations of the original relationships.

Implications

These findings suggest the following two recommendations for future mental health practice with Chinese-Americans:

First, more educational and outreach programs are needed--particularly with the male, older, less educated and foreign educated groups--in order to decrease the barriers to their receiving services and to improve their attitudes toward and knowledge about community mental health services.

Second, special programs such as ethnic advocacy, information services, and so on are needed to assist the male, older, less educated, and foreign educated groups of Chinese-Americans in their negotiations with the mental health system for more effective and responsive service delivery.

Implications for Future Research

From a review of the literature on mental health and mental illness, two general questions were formulated about utilization of mental health services. First, what do Chinese-Americans define as mental illness and how do they cope with it when it occurs? Second, what kinds of knowledge and attitudes do Chinese-Americans have about mental health services, and what barriers do they perceive to their receiving such services?

This study not only provides some empirical evidence and answers to these questions, but also indicates a need for further research and changes in mental health policy. For instance, respondents with more Chinese traditional cultural orientations had more positive attitudes toward Western concepts of mental illness and its treatment, and yet they were discovered to be less knowledgeable about available services. Whether or not Chinese-Americans in other communities or parts of the nation might show the same attitudes is unknown. To answer this question, this study needs to be replicated with Chinese-Americans who live in different geographical areas of this country. Although this study was the first known empirical survey of Chinese-Americans' view of mental illness and mental health services, it is more of a contribution to breadth than depth of knowledge about how Chinese-Americans view their mental health. This study was restricted in scope to a random sample of households in New Chinatown of Los Angeles and has limitations in the generalizability of the findings. Like all exploratory-descriptive studies, this survey has not determined cause and effect relationships between Chinese cultural orientations and mental health judgments. The task of identifying such relationships is left to future researchers.

A need also exists for an empirical examination of the outcomes of mental health programs designed and administered by Chinese professionals and/or qualified bilingual Westerners. These outcomes should be compared to those of current programs. Such a study could not only provide a comparative result of the two programs but also reveal some insights into the relative effectiveness of specific treatment techniques and methods.

In conclusion, the results of this study have provided some insights into Chinese-Americans and mental illness and mental health services. Many issues and questions are raised in this study which require further study. Hopefully, the findings will lead to modifications in clinical practice and contribute to changes in mental health policy and program development. Also, it is hoped that this study will make a modest contribution to an expanding body of knowledge about Chinese-Americans and other ethnic minorities.

APPENDIX A

CENSUS DATA OF THE GEOGRAPHICAL AREA UNDER STUDY[a]

	Census Tract Number			
	197100		207100	
	No.	Percent	No.	Percent
Total population	1459	100.0	3232	100.0
Spanish (including Mexican-Americans)	674	46.2	885	27.4
Negro	5	0.3	9	0.3
American-Indian	2	0.1	6	0.2
Japanese	0	0.0	25	0.8
Chinese	757	51.9	2287	70.8
Korean	0	0.0	6	0.2
Filipino	9	0.6	4	0.1
Hawaiian	0	0.0	0	0.0
Others (including white)	12	0.8	10	0.3

[a]Information taken from and derived from the 1970 U.S. Census data.

APPENDIX B

CASE MATERIALS AND RESEARCH INSTRUMENTS

Census Tract # _____ Case # _____

Address _____ Los Angeles

Interviewer_____ Date _____ 1975

Language of Interview _____

       Good Morning (Afternoon or Evening). I am from the University
of Southern California, School of Social Work. I am visiting some of
the people in this neighborhood to learn of their opinions about certain
problems which may take place in their lives. I have a few questions
to confidentially ask you about such problems. Your answers as to what
you think about these problems will be very important to me, to various
programs, and the helping professions. It will probably take about thirty
minutes of your time to answer these questions. Your assistance in this
matter will be greatly appreciated. As I said earlier, I am not interested
in your name, and your answers will be strictly protected from any identification with you.

Part I

       Now, I would like to tell you about four imaginary persons and
ask you a few questions about them

<u>Case I:</u>

"I am thinking of a man--let's call him Andrew Chao-- who is very suspicious: he doesn't trust anybody, and he's sure that everybody is against him. Sometimes he thinks that people he sees on the street are talking about him or following him around. A couple of times, now, he has beaten up men who didn't even know him. The other night, he began to curse his wife terribly, he said, she was working against him, too, just like everybody else."

1. Would you say that there is anything wrong with this man or not?

    _____Yes (to question 2)
    _____No (to question 3)

2. If yes, would you say this man, Andrew Chao, has some kind of mental illness or not?

    _____Yes

    _____No   (to question 3)

    If yes, how serious is his mental illness?

    _____Extremely serious

    _____Moderately serious

    _____Mildly serious

    _____Not serious at all

3. What do you think makes him act this way? Or in other words, what is causing him to act like this?

4. If someone in your family had this problem, where would you go for help?

    (Is there anything else you would do?)

5. Do you personally know any Chinese who shows this kind of behavior? Or acts like this man?

    _____Yes

    _____No

    _____Don't know

<u>Case II</u>:

   "Now here's a young woman in her twenties, let's call her
Beverly Chien. She has never had a job, and she doesn't seem to want
to go out and look for one. She is a very quiet girl, she doesn't even
talk much to her own family, and she acts like she is afraid of people,
especially young men her own age. She won't go out with anyone, and
whenever someone comes to visit her family, she stays in her own room
until they leave. She just stays by herself and daydreams all the
time, and shows no interest in anything or anybody."

6. Would you say that there is anything wrong with this woman or not?

_____Yes (to question 7)
_____No (to question 8)

7. If yes, would you say this woman, Beverly Chien, has some kind of
   mental illness or not?

_____Yes
_____No (to question 8)

If yes, how serious is her mental illness?

_____Extremely serious
_____Moderately serious
_____Mildly serious
_____Not serious at all

8. What do you think makes her act this way? Or in other words,
   what is causing her to act like this?

9. If someone in your family had this problem, where would you go for
   help?

   (Is there anything else you would do?)

10. Do you personally know any Chinese who shows this kind of behavior?
    Or acts like this woman?

_____Yes
_____No
_____Don't know

<u>Case III:</u>

Here's a different sort of girl, let's call her Elizabeth Chow. She seems happy and cheerful. She's pretty, has a good job, and is engaged to marry a nice young man. She has loads of friends: Everyone likes her, and she's always busy and active. However, she just can't leave the house without going back to see whether she left the gas stove lit or not. And she always goes back again just to make sure she locked the door. And one other thing about her; she's afraid to ride up and down in elevators; she just won't go any place where she has to ride in an elevator to get there."

11. Would you say there is anything wrong with this woman or not?

_____Yes (to question 12)

_____No (to question 13)

12. If yes, would you say this woman, Elizabeth Chow, has some kind of mental illness or not?

_____Yes

_____No (to question 13)

If yes, how serious is her mental illness?

_____Extremely serious

_____Moderately serious

_____Mildly serious

_____Not serious at all

13. What do you think makes her act this way? Or in other words, what is causing her to act like this?

14. If someone in your family had this problem, where would you go for help?

(Is there anything else you would do?)

15. Do you personally know any Chinese who shows this kind of behavior? Or acts like this woman?

_____Yes

_____No

_____Don't know

Case IV:

"Now, I'd like to describe a twelve-year-old boy--Frederick Wu. He's bright enough and in good health, and he comes from a comfortable home. But his father and mother have found out that he's been telling lies for a long time now. He's been stealing things from stores, and taking money from his mother's purse, and he has been playing truant, staying away from school whenever he can. His parents are very upset about the way he acts, but he pays no attention to them."

16. Would you say that there is anything wrong with this young man or not?

_____Yes (to question 17)

_____No (to question 18)

17. If yes, would you say this young man, Frederick Wu, has some kind of mental illness or not?

_____Yes

_____No (to question 18)

If yes, how serious is his mental illness?

_____Extremely serious

_____Moderately serious

_____Mildly serious

_____Not serious at all

18. What do you think makes him act this way? Or in other words, what is causing him to act like this?

19. If someone in your family had this problem, where would you go for help?

(Is there anything else you would do?)

20. Do you personally know any Chinese who shows this kind of behavior? Or acts like this young man?

_____Yes

_____No

_____Don't know

Part II

Now, I am going to read some statements to you, and I would like to know if you agree or disagree with each one.

	Strongly Agree	Agree	Neither Agree/Disagree	Disagree	Strongly Disagree
21. Mental illness is usually inherited.	___	___	___	___	___
22. Chinese medicine is very effective in treating persons with mental illness.	___	___	___	___	___
23. Mental illness usually is brought on as punishment for sins.	___	___	___	___	___
24. Counseling and psychotherapy are very effective in treating persons with mental illness.	___	___	___	___	___
25. Mental illness usually arises from lack of willpower.	___	___	___	___	___
26. Mental illness usually comes from tensions and troubles in the family.	___	___	___	___	___
27. A person who has a mental illness is likely to recover faster if he is with his family	___	___	___	___	___
28. Western medicine is very effective in treating persons with mental illness.	___	___	___	___	___
29. If the living environment is really bad, e.g., not enough money, no job, etc. anyone can become mentally ill.	___	___	___	___	___
30. Mental illness is usually curable.	___	___	___	___	___

Part III

The following questions are related to your attitudes and knowledge about mental health services and resources:

31. Do you have health insurance?

    _____Yes
    _____No

    If yes, does your health insurance cover mental health services?

    _____Yes
    _____No
    _____Don't know

32. Do you know of any mental health agencies or clinics where someone from this neighborhood could go for help? (<u>Check all that apply</u>.)

	Respondent Identified	Respondent Recognized	
		Yes	No
Resthaven Community Mental Health Center	_____	____	____
County South Central Mental Health Services	_____	____	____
LAC-USC Medical Center, Psychiatric Unit	_____	____	____
Others (specify)	_____	____	____

33. Are these clinics or agencies close enough for people of this neighborhood to get there for services without much difficulty?

    _____Yes
    _____No
    _____Don't know

34. In general, how do you think Chinese people are treated at these mental health clinics or agencies?

    _____Good
    _____Fair
    _____Poor

35. In general, do you think a mental health clinic or agency can really help Chinese who have mental or family problems?

_____Yes

_____No

_____Don't know

36. Would you encourage a friend or neighbor to go to a mental health clinic or agency if he had a mental or family problem?

_____Yes

_____No

37. Would you encourage a relative or family member to go to a mental health clinic or agency if he had a mental or family problem?

_____Yes

_____No

38. Would you go to a mental health clinic or agency if you had a mental or family problem?

_____Yes

_____No

39. Have you ever used services at any of these mental health clinics or agencies?

_____Yes

_____No

40. Do you know any Chinese who has used services at any of these mental health clinics or agencies?

_____Yes

_____No

41. Do you think most Chinese would avoid going to mental health clinics or agencies even when they were in need of help?

_____Yes

_____No

42. What kinds of problems do you think Chinese may face by going to mental health clinics and agencies? (Check all that apply.)

_____Communication (language) problem

_____Financial (money) problem

_____Moral (shame or losing face) problem

_____Information (don't know where to go) problem

_____Others (specify)_____

43. Based on your opinion what would be the ideal methods in treating Chinese mental patients?

Part IV

44. How often do you celebrate Chinese festivals, such as Lunar New Year, Tomb festival, Mid-Autumn festival, and so on?

_____Very often

_____Often

_____Sometimes

_____Rarely

_____Never

45. How often is English spoken in this house?

_____Very often

_____Often

_____Sometimes

_____Rarely

_____Never

46. How often do you eat Chinese meals at home?

_____Very often

_____Often

_____Sometimes

_____Rarely

_____Never

47. How well can you speak Chinese?

_____Very well
_____Fairly well
_____Fair
_____A little bit
_____Not at all

48. How well can you speak English?

_____Very well
_____Fairly well
_____Fair
_____A little bit
_____Not at all

49. How often do you read Chinese newspapers, magazines, etc.?

_____Very often
_____Often
_____Sometimes
_____Rarely
_____Never

50. How often do you read English newspapers, magazines, etc.?

_____Very often
_____Often
_____Sometimes
_____Rarely
_____Never

51. How many of your friends are Chinese?

_____All of them
_____Most of them
_____Some of them
_____Very few of them
_____None of them

52. How many of your friends are Americans?

_____All of them
_____Most of them
_____Some of them
_____Very few of them
_____None of them

53. How often do you go to places outside of Chinatown?

_____Rarely or never
_____Few times a year
_____Few times a month
_____Few times a week
_____Everyday

54. How often do you do your grocery shopping at the stores in Chinatown?

_____Very often
_____Often
_____Sometimes
_____Rarely
_____Never

55. How often do you buy your other commodities at the stores in Chinatown?

_____Very often
_____Often
_____Sometimes
_____Rarely
_____Never

56. Living in Chinatown makes you feel secure and less frightened.

_____Strongly agree
_____Agree
_____Uncertain
_____Disagree
_____Strongly disagree

57. It is necessary to send our children to Chinese language school so that they will not forget about their Chinese culture and identity.

_____Strongly agree

_____Agree

_____Uncertain

_____Disagree

_____Strongly disagree

58. Whenever we have serious emotional and living problems we should go to our family members or relatives for help first.

_____Strongly agree

_____Agree

_____Uncertain

_____Disagree

_____Strongly disagree

59. We should consider governmental agencies and professionals as the major resources to get help for our serious emotional and living problems.

_____Strongly agree

_____Agree

_____Uncertain

_____Disagree

_____Strongly disagree

Part V

Now, I would like to ask you some questions about yourself.

60. Sex:

_____Male

_____Female

61. Age at last birthday: _____years

62. Place of birth:

_____American born
_____Foreign born

63. If American born, you are:

_____First generation
_____Second generation
_____Third generation
_____Fourth generation

64. If foreign born, you have lived in the United States for

_____years.

65. Marital status:

_____Married
_____Separated
_____Divorced
_____Widowed
_____Single, never married

66. If married, is your spouse employed?

_____Yes
_____No

67. Are you employed?

_____Yes
_____No

68. What is your occupation? _____

118

69. Major source of income:

_____Employment
_____Retirement
_____Social security
_____Public assistance
_____Others (specify)

70. What was your family's gross income last year?

_____Less than $3,000
_____$3,000 to $5,999
_____$6,000 to $9,999
_____$10,000 to $14,999
_____$15,000 to $19,999
_____$20,000 to $24,999
_____$25,000 or more

71. Do you rent_____ or own _____ this house (apartment)?

72. Education: Total years _____

_____United States, _____years
_____China, _____years
_____Hong Kong, _____years
_____Taiwan, _____years
_____Others (specify) _____years

73. Religion:

_____Ancestor worship
_____Buddhist
_____Protestant
_____Catholic
_____None
_____Others (specify) _____

Again, thank you very much for your time and cooperation.

DISCRIMINATORY POWERS OF TEN ITEMS RELATED TO WESTERN CONCEPT OF MENTAL ILLNESS AND ITS TREATMENT

Items	Discriminatory Power[a]
Mental illness is usually inherited	1.52
Chinese medicine is very effective in treating persons with mental illness	1.13
Mental illness usually is brought on as punishment for sins	1.67
Counseling and psychotherapy are very effective in treating persons with mental illness	0.96
Mental illness usually arises from lack of willpower	1.40
Mental illness usually comes from tensions and troubles in the family	0.56
A person who has a mental illness is likely to recover faster if he is with his family	1.26
Western medicine is very effective in treating persons with mental illness	0.42
If the living environment is really bad, e.g., not enough money, no job, etc. anyone can become mentally ill	0.32
Mental illness is usually curable	0.13

[a]0.50 was set as the minimum accepting level.

DISCRIMINATORY POWERS OF SIXTEEN ITEMS RELATED TO TRADITIONAL CHINESE CULTURAL ORIENTATION

Items	Discriminatory Power[a]
Celebrate Chinese festivals	0.68
Speak English in the house	2.37
Eat Chinese meals at home	0.78
Chinese linguistic ability	1.31
English linguistic ability	3.21
Read Chinese newspapers, magazines, etc.	2.11
Read English newspapers, magazines, etc.	3.22
Number of Chinese friends	1.30
Number of American friends	1.97
Go to places outside of Chinatown	2.31
Do grocery shopping in Chinatown	1.39
Buy other commodities in Chinatown	1.34
Feel secure and less frightened in Chinatown	0.80
Send children to Chinese language school	1.29
Go to family members or relatives for help	1.04
Get help from governmental agencies or professionals	0.15

[a]0.50 was set as the minimum accepting level.

BIBLIOGRAPHY

Books

Allport, Gordon. _The Nature of Prejudice_. New York: Doubleday & Co., 1958.

Bancroft, H. H. _History of California, 1860-1890_. San Francisco: Bancroft and Co., 1895.

_____. _Bancroft's Works_. Vol. 38. San Francisco: The History Co., 1890.

Babbie, Earl R. _Survey Research Methods_. Belmont, Ca.: Wadsworth Publishing Co., Inc., 1973.

Brown, Timothy; Stein, Kenneth; Huang, Katherine; and Harris, Darrel. "Mental Illness and the Role of Mental Health Facilities in Chinatown." In _Asian-Americans: Psychological Perspectives_. Edited by S. Sue and N. Wagner. Palo Alto, Ca.: Science & Behavior Books, 1973.

Clark, Margaret. _Health in the Mexican-American Culture_. University of California Press, Ltd., 1970.

Daniels, Roger. _Racism in California_. New York: The Macmillan Co., 1972.

DeGrazia, Sebastian. _Errors of Psychotherapy_. New York: Doubleday & Co., 1952.

Fenlanson, Anne T. _Essentials in Interviewing_. New York: Harper & Row Publishers, 1962.

Finestone, Samuel. _Community Mental Health Services in New York City_. New York: Center for New York City Affairs, 1973.

Fong, Stanley L. "Identity Conflicts of Chinese Adolescents in San Francisco," In _Minority Group Adolescents in the United States_. Edited by E. Brody. Baltimore: Williams & Wilkins, 1968.

Frank, Jerome D. "The Dynamics of the Psychotherapeutic Relationship." In _Mental Illness and Social Processes_. Edited by Thomas J. Scheff. New York: Harper & Row Publishers, 1967.

Goode, William J., and Hatt, Paul K. _Methods in Social Research_. New York: McGraw-Hill Book Co., 1952.

122

Hatanaka, Herbert; Watanabe, Bill Y.; and Ono, Shin'ya. "The Utilization of Mental Health Services by Asian Americans in Los Angeles Area." In Service Delivery in Pan Asian Communities. Edited by Wesley H. Ishikawa and Nikki Hayashi Archer. San Diego: Pacific Asian Coalition Mental Health Training Center, 1975.

Hitell, Theodore H. History of California. San Francisco: N. J. Stone and Co., 1897.

Kahn, Alfred J. Studies in Social Policy and Planning. New York: Russell Sage Foundation, 1969.

Kendall, Patricia L., and Lazarsfeld, Paul F. "Problems of Survey Analysis," In Continuities in Social Research. Edited by Robert K. Merton and Paul F. Lazarsfeld. Glencoe, Ill.: Free Press, 1950.

Kramer, Bernard M. "Racism and Mental Health as a Field of Thought and Action." In Racism and Mental Health. Edited by Willie, et al. Pittsburgh: University of Pittsburgh Press, 1973.

Kung, S. W. Chinese in American Life. Seattle: University of Washington Press, 1962.

Miller, Stuart Creighton. The Unwelcome Immigrant. Berkeley: University of California Press, 1969.

McLeod, Alexander. Pigtails and Gold Dust. Caldwell, Idaho: The Cazton Printers, Ltd., 1947.

Meany, E. S. History of the State of Washington. New York: The Macmillan Co., 1909.

Redlich, Fredrick C., and Freedman, Daniel X. The Theory and Practice of Psychiatry. New York: Basic Books, Inc., 1966.

Rosen, H., and Frank, J. "Negroes in Psychotherapy." In Mental Health of the Poor. Edited by F. Riessman, et al. New York: Free Press, 1964.

Selltiz, Claire; Jahoda, Marie; Deutsch, Morton; and Cook, Stuart W. Research Methods in Social Relations. New York: Holt, Rinehart and Winston, 1959.

Sue, Stanley, and Sue, Derald Wing. "Chinese-American Personality and Mental Health." In Asian-Americans: Psychological Perspectives. Edited by S. Sue and N. Wagner. Palo Alto, Ca.: Science & Behavior Book, Inc., 1973.

Sung, Betty Lee. Mountain of Gold. New York: The Macmillan Co., 1967.

Articles in Journals

Baker, John, and Wagner, Nathaniel. "Social Class and
    Treatment in Child Psychiatry Clinic." The Archives of
    General Psychiatry 14 (February 1966): 129-133.

Berk, Bernard B., and Hirata, Lucie Cheng. "Mental Illness
    Among the Chinese: Myth or Reality?" Journal of Social
    Issues 29 (1973): 149-166.

Bloch, Julia B. "The White Worker and the Negro Client in
    Psychotherapy." Social Work 13 (April 1968): 36-42.

Briar, Scott. "Use of Theory in Studying Effects of Client
    Social Class on Student's Judgments." Social Work 6
    (July 1961): 91-97.

Brill, Norman Q., and Storrow, Hugh. "Social Class and
    Psychiatric Treatment." The Archives of General
    Psychiatry 3 (October 1960): 340-344.

Chen, Pei-Ngor. "The Chinese Community in Los Angeles," Social
    Work 15 (December 1970): 591-598.

Cumming, Elaine and Cumming, John. "Affective Symbolism,
    Social Norms, and Mental Illness." Journal of Psychiatry 19
    (February 1956): 77-85.

Curry, Andrew E. "The Negro Worker and the White Client."
    Social Casework 45 (March 1964): 131-136.

Dohrenwend, Bruce P.; Bernard, Viola W.; and Kolb, Lawrence C.
    "The Orientation of Leaders in an Urban Area Toward
    Problems of Mental Illness." The American Journal of
    Psychiatry 118 (February 1962): 683-691.

Fibush, Esther. "The White Worker and the Negro Client."
    Social Casework 46 (May 1965): 271-277.

Fisher, Joel, and Miller, Henry. "The Effect of Client Race
    and Social Class on Clinical Judgments." Clinical Social
    Work 1 (Summer 1973): 100-109.

Harrison, Saul; McDermatt, John; Wilson, Paul; and Schrager,
    Jules. "Social Class and Mental Illness in Children:
    Choice of Treatment." The Archives of General Psychiatry 13
    (November 1965): 411-416.

Karno, Marvin, and Edgerton, Robert B. "Perception of Mental
    Illness in a Mexican-American Community." The Archives
    of General Psychiatry 20 (February 1969): 233-238.

Kim, Bok-Lim. "Asian-Americans: No Model Minority." Social
    Work 18 (May 1973): 44-53.

Kitano, Harry, and Sue, Stanley. "The Model Minorities."
    Journal of Social Issue 29 (1973): 1-9.

Kluckhohn, Florence Rochwood. "Family Diagnosis. I.
    Variations in the Basic Values of Family System" Social
    Casework 39 (February-March 1958): 66-69.

Lemkau, Paul V., and Crocetti, Guido M. "An Urban Population's
    Opinion and Knowledge About Mental Illness." The American
    Journal of Psychiatry 118 (February 1962): 692-700.

Lief, Harold; Lief, Victor; Warren, Charles; and Heath, Robert.
    "Low Dropout Rate in a Psychiatric Clinic: Special
    Reference to Psychotherapy and Social Class." The Archives
    of General Psychiatry 5 (August 1961): 200-211.

Parsons, Talcott. "Illness and Role of Physician: A Socio-
    logical Perspectives." American Journal of Orthopsychiatry 21
    (July 1951): 452-460.

Sarbin, Theodore R., and Mancuso, James. "Failure of a Moral
    Enterprise: Attitudes of the Public Toward Mental Illness,"
    Journal of Counseling and Clinical Psychology 35
    (October 1970): 159-173.

Simmons, Leonard C. "Crow Jim: Implications for Social Work."
    Social Work 8 (July 1963): 24-30.

Sue, Stanley, and Mckinney, Herman. "Asian-American Clients
    in the Community Mental Health System." American Journal
    of Orthopsychiatry 45 (January 1975): 111-118.

Wright, Beryl R. "Social Aspects of Change in the Chinese
    Family Pattern in Hong Kong." Social Psychology 63
    (January 1964): 31-39.

Yamamoto, Joe, and Goin, Marcia K. "Social Class Factors
    Relevant for Psychiatric Treatment." Journal of Nervous
    and Mental Disease 142 (April 1966): 332-339.

_____; James, Quinton; Bloombaum, Milton; and Hattem,
    Jack. "Racial Factors in Patient Selection." American
    Journal of Psychiatry 124 (November 1967): 630-637.

Public Documents

City of Los Angeles. "The State of the City: A Cluster
Analysis of Los Angeles." Los Angeles City Community
Analysis Bureau, June 1974.

County of Los Angeles, Department of Health Services.
Discharge and Units of Services by Ethnic Origin: Fiscal
Year 1973-1974, Vol. 3, No. 11. Los Angeles: County
Department of Health Services, Mental Health Research
and Evaluation Division, October 16, 1975.

State of California. Mental Health Laws. Sacramento:
Department of Mental Hygiene, 1970.

U.S. Department of Commerce, Bureau of the Census. Census
of the United States, 1830-1880: Population.

_____. Census of the United States, 1890: Population.

_____. Census of the United States, 1920: Population.

_____. Census of the United States, 1930: Population.

_____. Census of the United States, 1970: Population.

_____. United States Census of Population: 1970,
vol. 1, Characteristics of the Population, California.

U.S., Department of Health, Education, and Welfare. A Study
of Selected Socio-Economic Characteristic of Ethnic
Minorities Based on the 1970 Census, vol. 2:
Asian-Americans. Prepared by Urban Associates, Inc.,
Arlington, Va., July 1974.

Unpublished Materials

Ballislilla, Roger M. "Utilization of Preventive-Diagnostic
Services Among Late Adulthood Persons." New York: Center
for Housing and Environmental Studies, Cornell University,
February 1969.

Chen, Peter Wei-teh. "Cultural Conflict and Mental Illness:
A Case Study of a Mentally Ill Chinese-American Patient."
M.S.W. thesis, California State University, Fresno,
June 1968.

Chen, Wen-Hui Chung. "Changing Socio-Cultural Patterns of the Chinese Community in Los Angeles." Ph.D. dissertation, University of Southern California, June 1952.

Greater Los Angeles Community Action Agency, Research and Evaluation Division. "Ethnicity of Los Angeles County Population, April 1974." (Mimeographed.)

Haase, W. "Research Diagnosis, Socioeconomic Class and Examiner Bias." Ph.D. dissertation, New York University, 1956.

Hollingshead, August B. "The Two Factor Index of Social Position." New Haven, Conn., 1957. (Mimeographed.)

Lee, Ivy. "A Profile of Asians in Sacramento." U.S. Department of Health, Education, and Welfare Grant No. IROIMH 21086-01, September 30, 1973.

Padell, Lawrence. "Studies in the Use of Health Services by Families on Welfare: Utilization of Preventive Health Services." New York: The Center for Study of Urban Problems, 1969.

Roberts, Robert W. "A Study of Social Workers' Judgments of Child Abuse." D.S.W. dissertation, Columbia University, 1970.

Star, Shirley A. "The Public's Ideas about Mental Illness." Paper presented at the meeting of the National Association of Mental Health, Indianapolis, Indiana, November 5, 1955.

Sue, Stanley, and Sue, Derald. "The Reflection of Cultural Conflict in the Psychological Problems of Chinese Americans." Paper presented at the First National Conference on Asian American Studies, Los Angeles, California, April 1971.

Wu, Frances Yu-ching. "Mandarin-speaking Aged Chinese in Los Angeles Area: Social Services and Needs." D.S.W. dissertation, University of Southern California, June 1974.

Other Sources

Giordano, J. Ethnicity and Mental Health: Research and
    Recommendations, National Project on Ethnic American of
    American Jewish Committee, 1973.

National Association of Social Workers, Encyclopedia of Social
    Work. New York: NASW, 1965.

The Columbia Encyclopedia. 3d ed. New York: Columbia
    University Press, 1962.